CREATING
REAL
WEALTH

MICHAEL KEMP

Hardback edition published in 2010 by IQ Investing
Paperback edition published in 2018
© Michael Kemp 2010, 2018
The moral rights of the author have been asserted

 A catalogue record for this
book is available from the
NATIONAL
LIBRARY National Library of Australia
OF AUSTRALIA

ISBN: 978-0-6482387-4-4

Editorial & Project Management by Major Street Publishing Pty Ltd
Internal design by Production Works
Cover design by Rob Cowpe Design
Printed in Australia by Griffin Press

10 9 8 7 6 5 4 3 2 1

Disclaimer
The material in this publication is of the nature of general comment only, and does not represent professional advice. It is not intended to provide specific guidance for particular circumstances and it should not be relied on as the basis for any decision to take action or not take action on any matter which it covers. Readers should obtain professional advice where appropriate, before making any such decision. To maximum extent permitted by law, the author and publisher disclaim all responsibility and liability to any person, arising directly or indirectly from any person taking or not taking action based upon the information in this publication.

For Andrew and Jessica

ABOUT THE AUTHOR

Dr. Michael Kemp completed an MBA before embarking on a career in corporate finance during the mid–1980s bull market. As a young financier he was awarded the Ian Roach Prize for achieving first place nationally among employees of the Australian Securities Exchange studying for the Graduate Diploma in Applied Finance and Investment.

Michael Kemp graduated from Melbourne University and has subsequently gained two master's degrees, including an MBA from Monash University.

His financial career has included working in the Treasury Department of the Australian Wheat Board, as a trader for Bankers Trust and in the Corporate Finance department of stockbroking firm Potter Warburg (both in Australia and London).

Today Michael spends his time investing on his personal account, writing articles for the Australian Securities Exchange and analyzing and writing about stocks for the Barefoot Blueprint newsletter.

To Michael, finance has always been a passion, never a job.

CONTENTS

FOREWORD BY COLIN NICHOLSON

Man's mind, once stretched by a new idea,
never regains its original dimensions.

OLIVER WENDELL HOLMES (1809–1894)

Before considering whether to read this book it is necessary to give a warning. This is a dangerous book. It has the potential to change the way you design your life. There is a great risk that by reading it you will be exposed to ideas that will make you wealthier, both financially and in terms of happiness with your life. If you feel that you want to take that risk, read on.

Let me tell you about Jason and his wife Elizabeth. They are in their late twenties, employed and considering marriage. Elizabeth owns an apartment with a large mortgage and Jason owns a car using a loan he is still paying off. Both of them have credit card debts and just manage to scrape together the minimum monthly payments. However, they enjoy life and with two incomes they purchase most things they want and have expensive holidays.

Nevertheless, as they consider marriage, they begin to worry about what is ahead of them. Can they cope financially? As they struggle to bring up a family, will they have to give up the little pleasures in life, which it seems only money can bring?

They look first at their own parents and at their friends and their parents. No matter how hard they look, they cannot find a role model because all of these people are in the position of living hand-to-mouth, while working hard and long hours. Some have second jobs. It seems to them that this is the only way forward.

Then one day, Jason takes Elizabeth to visit his grandmother for the first time, on her birthday. As they come away from the visit, Elizabeth observes that Jason's grandmother seems to be financially secure in her retirement and is one of the most contented and happy people she has ever met.

After tossing it around between them, they decide to see Jason's grandmother again and ask for her advice about their future. To their pleasant surprise she is very receptive to their questions. The grandmother begins by commending them for asking. She wryly observes that her own children, including Jason's father, have never listened to her attempts to guide them.

She explains that most people just trust to luck. They hope that wealth and happiness will come out of the clouds one day. Perhaps a relative will leave them money and property. Then again they may win a lottery. These are the people who have no idea of how life operates and wonder how other people become wealthier and happier than they are.

Next, the grandmother explains that there are other people who probably know what they have to do, but never make the effort to design their lives in the manner that they wish for. In effect, these are the people who watch others become wealthier and happier, but suffer great regret at not having made the effort themselves.

Finally, she begins to talk about the people who engineer their lives so that they become wealthier financially and richer in the lives they lead in every respect. This book is here for you to notionally sit beside Jason and Elizabeth as the grandmother outlines to them what she has done with her own life. How she and her late husband became very comfortably wealthy and led lives that were rich in all the aspects of life which add up to happiness.

It is never too late to read *Creating Real Wealth*, which will take you through the four dimensions of wealth creation. However, the earlier you start the better. This is a book of untold value for people who seek a comfortable and satisfying life. It can become a blueprint for you to use to design a life that you will look back on with great satisfaction. Every parent should read it. Then they should pass it on to their children and grandchildren. This is best done when they are still young and have the optimistic and flexible outlook on life which children have as they grow to become adults.

AUTHOR PREFACE

Before commencing a career in finance in the 1980s my education had provided me with a belief that financial markets could be understood by developing skills in economics, accounting and mathematics. I innocently believed that, armed with this knowledge, I could set off and "beat the market". This belief was, however, not a universal one with academics of the time preaching a market theory termed the Efficient Market Hypothesis (EMH). The EMH proposes that the individual who believes he can gain an edge in the financial markets through knowledge and education is likely to be fooling himself since the markets can't be beaten. Proponents believe that markets react efficiently and immediately to information impossible to forecast.

In 1936, and well before the EMH was proposed, economist John Maynard Keynes expressed his opinion on our ability to profit from mathematical calculation with his comments having a very clear application to the financial markets:

> "human decisions affecting the future, whether personal or political or economic, cannot depend on strict mathematical expectation, since the basis for making such calculations does not exist."[1]

To me, however, it seemed that knowledge must provide an advantage. My conviction of this has strengthened, but my belief in what knowledge you must have to gain this edge has altered.

Perhaps the greatest revelation was my realisation that the factors which moved markets could not always be counted or measured. Economics and mathematics alone were not adequate to explain movements. I therefore looked increasingly to the complexity and irrationality of human thought as part of the mix. Not only did this appear to have an impact on the movement of markets, but I also found it an interesting study to observe how people reacted to the markets' gyrations.

There are spin-offs in the study of human behaviour. Not only does an understanding of the frailties of human decision-making help when investing, but it also assists in making life's broader decisions. Human thought and behaviour provide the common thread through this book. It is not just about making money in the stock market. It goes way beyond this single concept. Many people pin their hopes and dreams solely on anticipated returns from the financial markets. The notion that overall success will be achieved as the result of just one outcome (i.e. a good return) is rarely questioned — and it should be.

Financial texts focus principally on the making of money. It seems to be a given that this is all that the reader is seeking. This thinking is driven by what appears to be a largely unquestioned and near universal desire for "more". Even the Chinese who only decades ago were seen by the West as being beyond the influence of capitalism are now increasingly seeking to emulate the American lifestyle. All thought is about "getting on" both materially and financially. This thinking is not a new phenomenon, but it seems to have gained momentum more recently. America always seems to be implicated as the leader of the charge, but there is no shortage of would-be followers.

Creating Real Wealth was born as the result of my realisation that the singular goal of income and capital maximisation is open-ended and therefore unattainable. Very few people have the capacity to know when enough is enough. An unrealised goal can lead to perpetual frustration and many people live their lives this way. Hopefully, you will see in this book a balanced perspective on investment — one that allows achievement of goals rather than the all too often felt confusion, frustration, disappointment and failure experienced by many would-be investors.

Michael Kemp, January 2010

INTRODUCTION

There's an old saying that "telling isn't knowing, and knowing isn't doing". It reminds us that it is a long road from ignorance to success and that the simple possession of knowledge doesn't guarantee a favourable outcome. It reminds us that knowledge itself commonly fails to influence behaviour. Everybody knows that the key to losing weight is to eat less. Yet few who are overweight commit to this. Similarly those who smoke ignore the warnings that it is detrimental to their health. Consequently entire industries are based on providing support to individuals who are incapable of "doing it on their own". One of these industries, the financial planning industry, provides advice to investors yet, as is typical of human behaviour, this advice is not always taken.

Even assuming that you have a working knowledge of finance, there are countless emotional and psychological pitfalls that have the potential to prevent you from converting this knowledge into success. Most of these emotional shortcomings are not even appreciated by those who fall prey to them. Some of this comes from us being wired the wrong way, but social forces and influences are also at play.

There are any number of books on what you should do in order to achieve financial independence, but *Creating Real Wealth* addresses why many people fail even when armed with this information. In relating back to the saying "telling isn't knowing, and knowing isn't doing" it focuses on the "knowing isn't doing". *Creating Real Wealth* takes you into the minds of the wealth-builders describing the thought-processes that they have used to secure their own financial futures.

It has been said that there are only four things that you need to know about money:

1 How to earn it
2 How to save it
3 How to invest it
4 How to enjoy it.

To slip in any one of them guarantees overall failure. Very few people have the skills to undertake all four successfully, and this is mainly due to emotional and psychological shortcomings. The factors influencing each of the four vary and I explore them individually. This book therefore is divided into four sections:

1   Our socially-driven expectations of earning money

2   Our incapacity to save

3   The fears and emotions associated with investing

4   The barriers to enjoying our lives even after amassing enough capital to provide for financial independence.

It is important to stress that you will need to discover for yourself what constitutes financial success. This is because no one else can live your life for you. Have no doubt that money has a power in shaping how your life is experienced. But its mere attainment is not enough. Skill must be developed at all four levels of money management for overall success. To achieve such control will provide the opportunity for a better life, not only for yourself but also for those who love and depend upon you.

Part I:
Making Money

CHAPTER 1

What is this thing called money?

"Men of business in England do not ... like the currency question. They are perplexed to define accurately what money is: how to count they know, but what to count they do not know."

WALTER BAGEHOT

Coming up with a definition for money is about as difficult as catching water with your hands. Money means different things to different people. For most, it is an emotive word with its interpretation drawn from a complex mix of preconceptions. Many imagine what life would be like with more of it. Alternatively, fear can be induced from the thought of not having enough of it. It is not money itself which people think about but rather the impact of its possession or absence on their ability to consume and of what.

Those being pursued by creditors see money as relief from stress or conviction. The weary or dissatisfied employee sees it as relief from the tedium of work. The status-hungry see it as the opportunity to obtain more material trophies or, as American economist and sociologist, Thorstein Veblen described, pursue "conspicuous consumption".[2] The homesick migrant might see it as the chance to return to his or her homeland to embrace loved ones. Money therefore has different meanings for different people leading to many definitions.

Dictionary definitions of money are largely unsatisfactory. One describes money as "notes and coins serving as a store of value", but this definition has its limitations. Small pieces of metal and sheets of coloured paper only describe the object and therefore fail to convey

3

the word's full meaning. Additionally, money doesn't need to be represented by anything physical. It can be represented by numbers on an LCD screen, thrown around in cyberspace as it is transferred between bank accounts via internet links. As a number is made smaller on one person's or institution's screen, there is a commensurate increase in the size of a number on another screen.

Economists might define money as "a medium of exchange" or "a standard for measuring the relative worth of different goods and services". But ask anyone what their perception of money is and unless they are an economist neither of these two definitions is likely to spring to mind. In asking someone what they perceive when a television, washing machine, truck or telegraph pole is mentioned, there is a consistent image or response. But the word "money" is different. It can be seen as bestowing security, power, independence and social acceptance, but also is capable of evoking criminal behaviour causing people to thieve, embezzle and murder. A lack of it can result in cheating, lying and suicide. Arguments over it result in the break-up of friendships, families and marriages. It evokes the deep seated emotions of fear, envy, depression and greed. It causes people to endure pain, risk their life, work long hours in dissatisfying jobs and suffer harsh climatic and physical conditions in order to obtain it. It causes people to move house, to live away from loved ones and to forego what would otherwise be much more satisfying pursuits. No, money is not simply notes and coins or figures on screens. It is far more complex than that.

The Bible acknowledges that money is not inert, that it has an ability to evoke emotion and undesirable actions in man when it says:

"For the love of money is the root of all evils."

First letter of Paul to Timothy,
Chapter 6, Verse 10, The New Testament

In acknowledging the emotion it evokes, The New Testament states that it is not money itself which is the root of all evil but rather the love of it. It is man's response that is described as evil.

Emotions are induced by perceptions of what money can bring. Response to the word usually is about what could be done with more of it, or fears associated with not having enough. The word "money" acts as a trigger which releases emotions compiled from an amalgamation of hopes, dreams and fears.

For proof that the mere thought of not having enough money can induce bizarre behaviour consider the situation of the nineteenth century American speculator, Nathan Prime. Prime had become wealthy by successfully trading stocks, bonds and real estate. But despite this he committed suicide in 1832 because he was fearful that his speculative habits might one day result in the loss of his fortune and he didn't want to endure the social disgrace that would be associated with this possibility.

Money has enormous control over most of our lives. Few of us control it, rather it controls us. For most it determines what time to get up in the morning, what activities to undertake five days out of seven, what can and can't be said at work. It determines how to dress and how to behave. If these actions are fundamentally aligned with life's goals and beliefs, all usually is well. But, if misaligned, there is conflict — and this can result in stress and job dissatisfaction. Work is then endured rather than enjoyed. Debt needs to be serviced and self-imposed financial obligations met so that there is a need to remain unhappily employed rather than free to pursue more satisfying activities. Precious time and emotional energy is traded in exchange for more notes, coins and figures in electronic accounts. Joe Dominguez aptly described this as trading "life's energy".[3] As if unconcerned that personal time is finite, it is traded for a commodity usually disposed of carelessly and irrationally in a way that belies the difficulty in obtaining it in the first place.

The irony is that as keen as we are to have money, it is rarely held for long. The left hand receives it and the right hand spends it. Why then, is something that is so eagerly sought so quickly disposed of? In fact, many people spend it even before they obtain it, by purchasing on credit. Obviously, it is not money itself they seek but, rather, what money provides. Although money is necessary for food, clothing and shelter, it also buys trinkets, baubles and shiny objects that are held for a brief time and then discarded when they lose their shine. Money is exchanged for an endless stream of "stuff". Most of this "stuff" is bought for its attention-seeking power. But these purchased objects lose their value when they stop bestowing attention on their owner. Old or unfashionable items, previously valued objects, are discarded and new ones sought and bought to replace them.

What most people fail to realise is that the greatest benefits that money can provide actually come when it has been accumulated into a significant pool. And even those who realise this fact are often incapable of undertaking the process of accumulation. One of the principal forces working against them is their misdirected thinking. Thought is almost invariably directed towards earning more money, not on spending less of it. But the retention of what is already possessed is a powerful means by which money can be accumulated. By way of analogy imagine attempts to grow your bank balance as being similar to attempts to fill a bucket with water. If that bucket has a hole in its base the most rational solution to filling the bucket would be to plug the hole first, and not just to keep pouring larger amounts of water into it. But when money is flowing through the fingers of the financially irresponsible, they seek to earn more money, rather than to hold onto what they already have.

A more balanced and rational approach to managing money can provide enormous benefits in how life is spent. The way money is obtained, accumulated and used will have a profound effect on how time is spent and life, as a whole, is experienced. Common observations show that few people have the insight, skill or discipline to manage money well. However, these skills can be learned and, if put into practice, can be life changing.

As indicated in the introduction, to manage money successfully you need to be able to:

1   Earn it
2   Save it
3   Invest it
4   Enjoy it.

Most of us are preoccupied with the first of these to the detriment of the other three. But as will be discussed in this book, even if with a mind-boggling income, you ignore the last three points then you will ultimately be no better off financially than an unemployed busker. Indeed, as you read on, you will discover that if the lowest paid worker is following the last three points it is likely that he will end up wealthier than you could imagine.

By way of an example of our preoccupation with making more money as our sole solution to this dilemma let's look at a modern day parable.

The following is an adaptation of a story I came across on the internet several years ago. It describes a hypothetical person named Jack who lives an idyllic existence on a tropical beach. He has a simple but comfortable beach house close to the sand with beautiful views of the ocean. He has little accumulated financial wealth, but doesn't need much. Each morning he awakes and wanders along the beach to a nearby village. Well known to all the locals, he spends time talking to friends before walking to the end of the pier to catch fish. In the afternoon he exchanges some of his catch at the village square for basic necessities he can't produce himself. He then returns to his private beach for an afternoon swim and snooze on the warm sand. In the evenings he returns to the village where he socialises with his friends. Jack's life is uncomplicated and stress free.

Jack reaches 30 years of age and decides that he should "make more of his life". After a certain degree of self analysis he decides he should strike out on a career as a professional fisherman. So, instead of fishing only for his personal needs, he spends long hours each day fishing and subsequently selling his catch from a stall in the village. He no longer has time for friends or recreation. After 12 months he has saved enough to buy a fishing boat and within four years he has three more. Being a skilled fisherman, he eventually has a fleet of fishing boats, a staff of 100 and the largest fish processing plant in the southern hemisphere. He now lives in a large house in the middle of town. As business pressures grow he finds himself unable to spend any time at sea, let alone do anything outside of work in his office at the factory. He is driven by financial success yet has no idea of when "financial success" might be achieved.

One morning he is walking across the factory floor when he is stopped by one of his employees. "Jack," his employee asks, "I see you working 14 hours a day. You are like a man possessed. Why do you work so hard?"

Jack replies, "I'm saving for my retirement."

"What do you want to do when you retire?" asks the worker. Jack pauses before replying, "I'd like to live in a beach house on the other side of the island, fish from the pier and spend more time with my friends."

He once had that type of life. So ends this parable.

Money can make us behave in perverse ways; it can evoke emotion and it can distort values. You should always be conscious of this effect and try to find a balance that best serves real needs and beliefs rather than those defined by the "social norm". You should seek the wealth of life rather than material wealth.

When you hear the word "money", don't imagine like most people, that you need more. Don't immediately associate income with consumption because this will guarantee eternal poverty. In order to achieve financial success don't focus solely on making more, think also of how to save it, invest it and enjoy it.

CHAPTER 2

Beware the snake oil salesman

Snake oil — "a traditional Chinese medicine or an expression used metaphorically to describe any product with exaggerated marketing but questionable or unverifiable quality."

WIKIPEDIA

To be a better golfer, you would normally seek tuition from a golf pro and, in tennis, from a tennis pro. To enhance skills in making money, it would follow that you would seek advice from someone who is skilled at making a lot of it. Since many people see making lots of money as a desirable goal an industry has mushroomed to satisfy this demand. In fact, the demand is so strong that there is now an army of authors and speakers who have made their fortunes just through encouraging people to make their own fortune. But, if you look through the author or speaker's CV to see how they made their money, it often is through book sales and lecture fees. Do they have a financial skill? Probably not. Most of their skill is likely to be centred around marketing and public speaking. If a book is required and their writing skills are limited then "ghost-writers" do the work for them. However, if everyone tried to increase their income by giving lectures to others on how to increase their income then nothing would be produced and we would all be reduced to a mutual level of poverty.

What most of these "get rich quick" merchants are selling is hope. They talk a lot but the discussion is never about how the money is actually going to be generated. Rather, they talk/write about self-belief and a positive attitude. Work itself is often actually discouraged as it is linked with impeding financial progress. The ability to generate wealth is put forward as the ability to have a change of attitude. It's the old rah, rah type of message. You can do this! It's all up to you! They chant slogans like "if it's to be, it's up to me!" You've heard most of them before, but nothing is defined. There is no substance whatsoever. You leave a lecture all enthusiastic and starry-eyed and empty your wallet buying the book, CD or audio tape of what you have just heard. And, generally, it is all froth and bubble. Yet, encouraged by the speaker's claims of personal success, far too many hand over their credit cards. All they are doing is reinforcing in the speaker's mind, at least, his claims that wealth achievement is easy.

The enthusiasm usually fades soon after you return to daily life. The need to pay bills and the security of a regular pay cheque ends the starry-eyed dream. The motivational speaker might have warned against this mindset but, for most, the die is cast. The speaker usually is the only one who will end up making the money.

For many, these lectures represent a form of escapism similar to reading a novel or watching a movie. It provides short relief, but not an answer. And, when the enthusiasm fades and the dream turns to dust, there can be another downside — loss of self-esteem.

Although self-esteem is generated from multiple inputs, American psychologist William James has suggested that the two principal inputs are ability and expectations. He suggests that self-esteem is influenced directly by ability and, inversely, by increased expectations. Put simply, if you fail to achieve heightened expectations, your self-esteem will fall.

This does not mean you should not have a positive mental attitude and, in fact, there is plenty of evidence to indicate there is more chance of success when any task is approached with a positive outlook. But what you must be careful of here is holding enhanced expectations without means of execution. Often the motivational book or speech provides only half the story. It is then up to the reader or listener to provide the other half — converting the renewed enthusiasm into results. Without this the message is lost and the only measurable outcome is frustration and inadequacy. There must be a way for you to direct your new-found enthusiasm. You must act. Like a farmer who throws seed on barren ground, unless you have a vehicle for the execution of your enthusiasm then the desired result will not be achieved. Raised hope is not enough.

The pursuit of more money is not the only reason that these courses are attended. Many people are also unhappy in their jobs and they think that the speaker will provide them with a new direction. US research organisation Conference Board has found that 50 per cent of Americans in 2005 were dissatisfied with their jobs, up from 40 per cent in 1995. What would that rate be now? It is a scary thought. Internet search engine Google in February 2008, generated 6.7 million references when the words "work dissatisfaction" were keyed in. Little wonder, millions of "nine to fivers" around the world ask their work associates on Monday mornings: "How was your weekend?" And on Friday afternoon: "What are you doing this weekend?" Monday to Friday is so often endured for the enjoyment of the other two days in the week.

Motivational speakers and writers encourage us to leave our jobs as "only losers have jobs". The snake oil salesmen tell us "JOB stands for Just Over Broke". The impression is created that only entrepreneurs are capable of achieving financial independence. The fundamental mistake here is that income is just one part of gaining financial independence. The reality is that you do not have to be an entrepreneur or make outrageous sums of money to become financially independent. With the self-discipline of saving and the knowledge of the principles of investment, then financial independence can be achieved by almost anyone.

Clearly not all lecturers/writers on the subject of personal development are snake oil salesmen. An example is highly respected presenter Earl Nightingale (1921-1989) who is considered by many as the father of this type of presentation. Nightingale, a successful American radio and television personality, wrote and presented the radio show "Our Changing World" to a wide audience for more than 40 years. His approach was balanced with topics of discussion covering a broad range of issues. The show's popularity can be measured by the fact that it was aired five days a week on more than 1000 radio stations, attracting an audience of more than 40 million listeners. His massive audience not only reflected Nightingale's presentation style, but the degree to which Americans craved a new direction in their lives. Topics of discussion included creativity, happiness, interpersonal relationships and self-esteem. Nightingale received a gold record award for what was perhaps his best known recording — "The Strangest Secret". Basically, "The Strangest Secret" argued:

"We become what we think about."

Although Nightingale popularised the expression, it was far from a new concept. In fact, it had been around so long that it is surprising it was still referred to as a "secret". Nightingale acknowledged that men had long recognised the power of the mind in shaping individual destiny and provided quotes from numerous past politicians, philosophers and, indeed, The Bible itself.

The recording "The Strangest Secret" was inspired by the book *Think and Grow Rich* written by journalist and author Napoleon Hill.[4] First published in 1937, Nightingale had read the book as a young man. *Think and Grow Rich* has sold millions of copies and is still in print today. The book, 25 years in the making, is the distillation of the concepts of success as provided to the author from interviews with hundreds of prominent businessmen. Hill's first research interviews for the book were with American steel baron Andrew Carnegie. Others were with Thomas Edison, Henry Ford, J.D. Rockefeller and F.W. Woolworth. Although the secret of achievement is not directly defined by Hill, the concept of positive thought is the enduring theme.

Taken at face value this makes sense. How can anyone succeed at anything unless mentally committed? Taken to its opposite extreme, how can anyone who is severely depressed achieve anything when curled up in an embryonic form in bed unable even to start the day? Enthusiastic people, on the other hand, are initiators and leaders. Others follow their example in the hope they have the answer. But, as stated previously, if this thought is placed in the wrong mind it has the potential to undermine self-esteem.

An important point to make is that Earl Nightingale's words "You become what you think about" can be interpreted in more than one way and because of this could be open to misinterpretation. They could be read to mean that if you are dissatisfied with your present existence then be guided to pursue the existence that you think preferable. For example, the factory worker who dreams of owning a small business or the dentist who would rather be operating a plant nursery. Or put another way: "Follow your dreams". Nightingale often extolled the power of serendipity, that if you just take the first step and commit to the newly chosen existence you will succeed. This certainly could be the pathway for many who are dissatisfied with their current lives to pursue a better one. Unfortunately, however, most of us are too fearful of financial failure and therefore endure the security of the present, unhappy in our work. Basically, Nightingale suggested: conduct your life to balance your emotional needs rather than your imagined financial needs. And in pursuing this Nightingale would have added that in this way your financial needs will also be met — as a result of your actions, rather than as a driver of actions.

Nightingale might have extolled the benefit of leaving an unsatisfying career, but he wasn't suggesting this be based on a blind leap of hope or faith. Rather there needed to be a vocation in mind. He described the futility of tolerating a distasteful existence while craving another.

While it is possible to acknowledge the significant personal benefit from this interpretation of Nightingale's words "you become what you think about", there is another, less desirable interpretation. Although Nightingale's principal concern was for people to fulfil their lives at all levels, including emotionally and spiritually, others have focused solely on materialistic goals. Some therefore have interpreted his phrase as: "If you think hard enough about ways of making money, then you can make lots of it."

However, there is a real danger in this way of thinking. For example, you could pursue a certain career just because it offers high remuneration. This is to use the phrase "you become what you think about" as a form of brainwashing in the pursuit of making more money. This behaviour is often proposed in the books, tapes and CDs produced by the new age entrepreneurs. "Come join us." "Leave your dead-end job and become a financial success." "Stop thinking like a loser."

Yes, pursue dreams but not just for the sake of money. To yearn merely for more money and to sacrifice everything else in its pursuit is not a dream worth chasing.

The title of Napoleon Hill's book *Think and Grow Rich* has ensured that millions of people over several decades have plucked it from bookshelves around the world. A better title would have been "Think and Enjoy Your Life". But if this title had been used it is unlikely that sales would have been as brisk.

The power of positive thinking should not be underestimated, but it should not be used solely to boost your income at the expense of all other aspects of life. This is likely to lead to continued dissatisfaction, frustration and lack of personal fulfilment. Apply the power of positive thinking to all aspects of your life.

CHAPTER 3

Don't sacrifice the present

"Enjoy the process along with the proceeds,
because the process is where you live."

CHARLIE MUNGER

There is no escaping the fact that to function within modern society you must have some form of income. Unfortunately, for many this means "tolerating" a Monday to Friday job that provides little emotional fulfilment. As if that is not bad enough, the Monday to Friday sufferers compound their problem by committing either one or both of two all too common mistakes.

Firstly, they persist in their current existence in the expectation that life will be better when they stop what they are doing. The world's workforce is full of people dreaming of retirement. In putting their lives on hold until the age of 65, they are prepared to sacrifice half their life in the expectation that their last two decades — if they live that long — will be so special that it will compensate for four decades of dissatisfaction. As if failing to acknowledge mortality, the mind puts everything indefinitely into the future. Only the death of someone close reminds us that mortality is, in fact, a reality. To focus perpetually on the future is a mistake since we can only experience the present. American singer Janis Joplin reminded us of this in her well-known song, "Ball and Chain" when she said tomorrow never happens, "It's all the same day."

These thoughts have been on the minds of men and women for a long time.

Consider these words, translated from Sanskrit and significantly predating Christ:

> "Look well to this one day for it and it alone is life. In the brief course of this one day lie all the verities and realities of your existence: the pride of growth, the glory of action, the splendour of beauty. Yesterday is only a dream and tomorrow is but a vision. Yet each day, well lived, makes every yesterday a dream of happiness and each tomorrow a vision of hope."

The more of the present we enjoy, the greater our chances of structuring a life worth living.

Why do people put their lives indefinitely on hold telling themselves that one day it will all be better? It's not as if this is a conscious decision. It's most likely that the situation just crept up on them. A series of choices over a period of time sends them down a certain path until they realise one day that they are not where they want to be. They ultimately feel trapped because they have become "reliant" on the money they earn from their jobs. Insidious in its early progress, one day the sheer weight of its reality becomes too obvious to ignore. Unfortunately, all too often, the work being performed is not aligned with the individual's emotional needs and genuine interests. They dream of doing something else but feel trapped by the need to meet the constant flow of self-imposed financial responsibilities which characterise their lives. Some advice then to those who are at an early stage of their working career: if you are going to put yourself into a position of financial reliance then you had better make sure that you like your job.

For those who are presently enduring an unfulfilling existence in the hope of better times in the future consider the words of nineteenth century economist, John Stuart Mill:

> "Those only are happy who have their minds fixed on some object other than their own happiness — on the happiness of others, on the improvement of mankind, even on some act or pursuit followed not as a means but as itself an ideal end. Aiming thus at something else they find happiness by the way."[5]

Don't think of happiness as a goal. The actual achievement of any goal brings only short-lived satisfaction. More importantly, it is the *pursuit* of a meaningful goal that helps achieve long-lived happiness. Or put another way: it is not the pursuit of happiness, rather the happiness of pursuit. Therefore, when talking of a job the first rule is to pursue satisfying employment. The second rule you need to follow to avoid the second common mistake, is that if you don't like your job then don't try to compensate with excessive levels of consumption. You will actually bury yourself deeper as you are going to have to stay at your job to pay for it all. Michael Posner acknowledged this social contradiction when he stated the following:

"Our jobs may be boring, empty, and futile, but we have been indoctrinated to believe that compact discs and Armani suits can somehow fill the void."[6]

If you have any doubts regarding these issues then speak to elderly people, particularly to those who have sacrificed their lives in the pursuit of material wealth. People who know that their lives are drawing to a close will frequently be heard to say that they waited too long before they started living. That the sacrifice they made was not worth the outcome.

Many people live in two worlds. They live and work in one, yet they dream of another. Their notional world is one in which they imagine they are undertaking some activity they believe to be more enjoyable. It might be associated with a hobby or secondary skill. It might involve self-employment away from the will of an overpowering boss. It might involve outside activity for the office-bound worker or work in a more desirable climate or location.

For most there is a perceived barrier which prevents them from moving into the world in which they would rather live. Often they feel financially constrained. They have a job which provides a certain income, some of which might be used to service debt from prior expenditure. They are in an habitual pattern from which they are afraid to leave. They might be dissatisfied, but feel safe. To break away from this leaves them open to the fear of failure and to ridicule from peers. Although failure might be socially acceptable at the start of their working careers in their teens or early twenties, they fear the social stigma of financial failure when in their thirties, forties or fifties. They don't strive for personal advancement simply because they feel bound to their current lives.

The word serendipity is particularly relevant here. People tend to persist with what they know. They feel safety in what they can see rather than what may lie on the other side of that as yet unopened door. Opportunity is not pursued but, rather, there is a hope that it will be delivered on a plate. Serendipity acknowledges that opportunities usually arise only when you open the door and actually step through it. If the door opens into an arena of personal interest then the chance of success is high. For the cautious, this doesn't necessarily mean total rejection of current employment. The new interest initially could be pursued at nights or weekends. Even better, it might be possible to reduce the hours of current employment in order to free up time for the new. Effectively this means "dipping your toe in the water" before risking all and diving in.

Amazing changes in perception are likely if a move is successfully executed. Firstly, perceptions of the need for large amounts of money are likely to be tempered. Satisfaction is derived from the work itself, lessening the ill-perceived need for consumption as a surrogate for personal fulfilment. The need for compensation through high levels of income or the purchase of tokens of materialistic success becomes less important. Thoughts of retirement evaporate. Work becomes incorporated into your life rather than something that is endured and separated from life itself. If a person is passionate or interested in the work at hand then success is virtually guaranteed.

CHAPTER 4

More might not be the answer

"Men do not desire to be rich but to be richer than other men."

JOHN STUART MILL

Most people appear to spend their lives thinking of ways to make more money. They strike for it, dream of it, buy lottery tickets in the hope of winning it, attend courses on how to amass it, gamble for it, play the stock market and risk going to jail by stealing it. Yet it needs to be emphasised that where this behaviour is most prolific is within the wealthiest countries on the planet. Where then does it end? Is there an upper cap when it is declared that enough money is being earned? Unfortunately for most, the answer clearly is no. So let's look at a group of individuals who have had access to very large levels of income. Did it solve their problems? Did it satisfy their desires and so allow them to stop seeking more? Did it meet their emotional needs? Before starting this discussion it is important to note that each of the individuals mentioned had access to very high levels of income but never achieved a high level of accumulated capital (financial wealth). Or put another way, they earned a lot but their net worth never reflected this.

Rembrandt (1606-1669) is generally considered to have been one of Europe's greatest painters. Unlike some artists, whose skills are more fully recognised after their death, Rembrandt's ability was recognised at a young age. Credited as a skilled artist while still in his twenties, Rembrandt was regarded as a great painter over four decades of his life — and was rewarded with a large income. But, like many people today, Rembrandt never built significant wealth because he had a strong desire to consume. When the cash started flowing he moved to a prominent house, paid for through a big mortgage. He had a particularly strong taste for buying art, prints and rarities and lived beyond his means. Since his spending exceeded his income, he never accumulated any capital. Nor did he attempt to pay off any of his debt. At the age of 50, Rembrandt was declared bankrupt. His belongings and house were sold and, fortunately for his creditors, the sale proceeds covered his borrowings. Rembrandt died broke at 63 and was buried in an unmarked grave.

Mozart (1756-1791) arguably was the most famous composer of all time. He achieved success and acceptance at a young age and, in his twenties, was earning a substantial income. It could be said he was a pop star of his era. He sought a lifestyle "befitting" his income, renting an expensive apartment complete with fine furnishings and servants. However, his income declined in the latter half of the 1780s and his woes were compounded by the onset of war between Austria and Turkey in 1788. Mozart had no savings to fall back on and therefore found himself in financial trouble. To make up the shortfall he borrowed, mainly from a personal friend, Michael Puchberg. He was forced to move to cheaper lodgings and to curb his spending. Being accepted as a brilliant musician was not enough to counter his extreme anxiety which resulted from his dire financial position. Mozart died in 1791 at the age of 35.

American actor Debbie Reynolds, successful in her 50-year movie and television career, generated a substantial income. She was married and divorced three times — to singer Eddie Fisher, millionaire businessman Harry Karl and, finally, real estate developer Richard Hamlett. Yet despite her high profile life and exposure to income, property and wealth, Reynolds was forced to declare bankruptcy in 1997.

Another American movie and television actor, Burt Reynolds, filed for bankruptcy in late 1996. Despite a successful career that saw him as the number one box office attraction from 1978 to 1992, his ability to manage his personal finances did not match his acting skills.

Common weaknesses of many "stars" are excessive spending or poor investment decisions. American actor Kim Bassinger certainly suffered from the latter. In 1989 Bassinger paid $20 million for the small town of Braselton, Georgia, in the hope of establishing it as a tourist destination. The purchase was a financial drain hence the property was sold five years later when financial difficulties mounted through her decision to withdraw from the controversial film *Boxing Helena*. The studio sued as a result of her withdrawal and won an $8 million judgment against her. In 1993 Bassinger filed for bankruptcy, appealed the jury's decision and eventually settled for a lesser amount.

Another bankrupt entertainer was child actor Gary Coleman. As star of the US sit com series "Diff'rent Strokes" from 1978 to 1986, Coleman was, at one stage, the highest paid prime-time comedy actor on NBC, earning $70,000 an episode. His career earnings totalled $18 million. Coleman was 10 when he started the series and his parents therefore established a trust fund for his income payments. However, they named themselves as paid employees of Coleman's production company and siphoned off the money. Coleman eventually sued his parents and former manager over misappropriation of the funds but by the time a court dissolved the trust most of the money had gone.

As far as big spenders go, American "rapper" MC Hammer is up there with the best. Popular in the late 1980s and early 1990s, Hammer made more than $30 million from record sales. The trouble was that he spent more than this and in 1996 filed for bankruptcy declaring that he was $13 million in debt. He bought vast amounts of consumables and, like many entertainers, was never wealthy. Instead, he had a few years' access to a massive cash flow, only for this to slip through his fingers as quickly as it flowed in. And here's how he spent some of his earnings:

$12 million to build his home in Fremont, California which included:
- Recording studio
- 33-seat theatre
- Two swimming pools (one indoor, one outdoor)

- Tennis courts and a baseball diamond
- Waterfalls, ponds and aquariums
- Mirrored bathroom (at least $75,000 on mirrors throughout the house)
- $2 million of Italian marble floors and a floor-to-ceiling marble office
- Gold and marble Jacuzzi in the master bedroom
- Basketball courts
- Bowling alley
- 17-car garage
- $1.4 million spent on gold plated front gates.

Other MC Hammer purchases included:
- A fleet of 17 cars, including a Lamborghini, a stretch limousine, a Range Rover and a DeLorean
- Two helicopters
- $1 million worth of thoroughbred racehorses
- Antique golf clubs and Etruscan sculpture
- Gold chains for his four pet Rottweilers
- Extravagant parties
- A huge entourage of over 200 people, most of whom were on his payroll, for total monthly wages of $500,000
- A leased Boeing 727.

Clearly, this lifestyle could only continue for as long as he sold records and, when they didn't sell, his ship sank quickly.

Boxer Mike Tyson, the youngest man to have won a world heavyweight boxing title, was in his prime in the late 1980s and into the 1990s, capable of commanding $30 million for a night's work. During the course of his career Tyson earned more than $300 million yet in 2003 declared himself bankrupt with debts of $27 million. He was unable to manage his personal finances and possessed an incredible appetite for conspicuous consumption.

However, top of the pops in terms of the recent discussion has been singer Michael Jackson. He had a billionaire's taste for consumption on a millionaire's income and Jackson spent every dollar he ever earned, plus more.

It has been estimated that he earned more than $700 million during the course of his career, with income from recordings, concerts, music publishing, royalties through ownership of the Beatles catalogue, endorsements, merchandising and music videos. But Jackson managed to spend more than this and had to borrow heavily to make ends meet. He was spared bankruptcy only as the result of a decision which he made in 1985. In that year he bought ATV Music for $47.5 million. Its catalogue, which included 251 Beatles songs, appreciated significantly in value therefore allowing Jackson to use it as collateral to secure further loans.

In the spring of 2006 Jackson, again out of money, renegotiated his loan terms. A deal was struck between Jackson, Sony (co-owner of the Beatles catalogue) and lender Fortress Investments. At the time of the negotiations it was reported that Jackson's net worth was zero. In addition to his half share in the Beatles catalogue, Jackson's only other substantial assets were his Californian ranch, "Neverland", and a family home in Encino, both highly leveraged. In October, 2007, news broke that Jackson had defaulted on a $23 million loan secured against the ranch. The loan had expired on October 12 with papers being filed on October 22 in Santa Barbara County. Jackson's singing career was on the decline. He had spent approximately $1 billion over the course of his career and was now broke.

How could anyone spend $1 billion, yet have nothing to show for it? The answer is simple — living beyond one's means, whatever they might be. It was reported that before Jackson abandoned his "Neverland" ranch its annual running costs were about $2.5 million. His shopping expeditions were legendary. In the documentary "Living with Michael Jackson" it was shown how he frittered away $6 million within a matter of hours. The simple fact is that Jackson's spending was limited only by his earnings and what his bankers would lend him.

The examples of MC Hammer, Mike Tyson and Michael Jackson are extremely relevant since this type of behaviour is rife throughout society. The financial result is the same whether you are a high income earner or a salaried office worker — if you spend more than you earn you will be reduced to the same common denominator. Michael Jackson's financial behaviour was no different to a nine-to-five office worker who uses his or her lunch hour to load up the credit card with discretionary expenditure and is then unable to pay the money back. Take a couple of zeros off Jackson's dilemma and his pattern fits perfectly with the behaviour of countless others.

The point, and it is a very important one, is that an increased income is not the solution for imprudent financial behaviour. Sad but true, people who are financially stressed believe that a higher income will solve their problems. They fail to realise that it is not a lack of income but, rather, their spending that usually is the problem. Faced with a larger income they are more likely to use it for big spending rather than saving and investing. Reynolds, Bassinger, Coleman, Hammer, Tyson and Jackson were not born into wealthy families. Tyson was born in Brownsville, Brooklyn; Jackson one of nine children was born into relative poverty. All quickly developed the taste for conspicuous spending. A spender is a spender whether they have $100 in their pocket or $100,000.

An employee earning an annual salary of $100,000 who claims that he doesn't have the financial capacity to save is someone who is incapable of putting his life into perspective. Approximately one quarter of the world's population live on less than $1 per day. This group would see the person "existing" on $100,000 per annum in the same way the person on $100,000 per annum viewed Michael Jackson.

Try to explain to someone from Latin America, sub-Saharan Africa or the slums of Manila that spending $300 on a pair of sunglasses, $1,000 on a wrist watch, $50,000 on a motor car (or two) or the disposal of perfectly good clothes twice a year as fashions change is not behaving irrationally. The only reason that those in the industrialised world justify this behaviour is because so many other people in their social environment are behaving exactly the same way. They are all keeping up with the Joneses.

So let's look at the distribution of international income. Gross Domestic Product (GDP) per capita is often used as a financial scorecard enabling the construction of a league table to rate countries from wealthiest to poorest. Gross Domestic Product is a measure of the value of final goods and services produced in a country's economy. It is derived by adding the value of all domestically produced goods and services available for use which will not be used in further production. If divided by the nation's population, a figure is derived — GDP per capita which, rightly or wrongly, is presented as the theoretical allocated income per member of that nation. According to the International Monetary Fund Economic Database (April 2006) the United States, which comprises five per cent of the world's 6.5 billion people, is bettered on a GDP per capita basis by only one per cent of the world's population. Australia falls in closely behind the United States. The United States and Australia therefore constitute close to the wealthiest nations on earth. Despite this, some of the loudest cries of financial deprivation come from these countries. The wealthy are just not satisfied with what they already have. There clearly is a lack of recognition among the world's wealthy of when enough is enough. The goal of enough being "more than I have now" is the expectation of most.

In keeping with the widespread belief that more money paves the road to Nirvana, it is difficult for most to accept the concept that they might already actually be earning enough. Concepts of saving, investing and downsizing unrealistic consumption expectations appear to be far less attractive to the popular imagination than those of pay rises and lottery wins.

It is because of this common mindset that the book *The Millionaire Next Door* was met with surprise when released in 1996.[7] Authors Thomas Stanley and William Danko presented research undertaken to establish the demographics and habits of the typical US millionaire. They showed that the greater proportion of the millionaire population was made up of moderate income earners whose prudent behaviour with money had allowed them to accumulate significant capital. Further, they showed that conspicuous consumption was more likely to be an indicator of high debt than high net worth.

We tend to focus on consumption as an indicator of wealth. We see the clothes, the cars, the jewellery, the houses — all held up as symbols of economic well-being when the reality is that there is often no substance behind them. High consumption is often associated with a small bank balance. Texans have a saying for this behaviour — "Big hat, no cattle". Australians use the term "two dollar millionaires".

Stanley and Danko found that the common behavioural thread connecting the wealth accumulators was an ability to live within their means. They may not live in the best suburbs, they are unlikely to drive expensive cars, their material needs are modest but they don't necessarily compromise comfort. They are not misers and nor are they wasteful. They just seek value. By living within their financial means, surplus cash flow enables saving, investment and capital accumulation. The point that constantly came through in Stanley and Danko's research was that most of these people did not have stratospheric incomes. Their numbers weren't overly represented by entertainers, sports stars or high powered corporate leaders.

The media tends to focus its attention on two main groups. It both highlights people who earn a lot of money and those who consume conspicuously. Yet the first activity doesn't guarantee high net worth and the latter works directly against it. That observers often connect these activities with wealth only serves to reinforce their own financially inappropriate behaviour. They imagine their income to be inadequate when they compare it with that of an over-publicised minority group such as entertainers and sportspeople. They further compound their inability to achieve financial independence by emulating their consumption behaviour.

The simple reality is that given enough time and discipline, financial independence can be achieved even with relatively modest levels of income. That is, the levels of income derived by most people in the industrialised world. Examples of how financial independence can be achieved on modest income levels will be developed later in the book.

The essential message is that you do not need the income of a movie star to achieve financial independence. There is no need to aspire to winning the lottery or to fall under the trance of the promoter of a get-rich-quick scheme. In terms of income, everything you need is probably already in place. Unless you acknowledge the need to save, to invest and to enjoy your life, then believing that simply earning more money is the answer to your predicament will gain you the same degree of success as you could expect from betting on a thoroughbred racehorse that has only one leg.

Part II:
Saving Money

CHAPTER 5

Why save at all?

"The way to wealth, if you desire it, is as plain as the way to market. It depends chiefly on two words, industry and frugality; that is, waste neither time nor money, but make the best use of both. Without industry and frugality nothing will do, with them everything. He that gets all he can honestly and saves all he gets will certainly become rich ... "

BENJAMIN FRANKLIN

"All kinds of people ask me for some foolproof system for achieving financial security or saving for their retirement ... Spend less than you make; always be saving something. Put it into a tax-deferred account. Over time it will begin to amount to something. THIS IS SUCH A NO BRAINER."

CHARLIE MUNGER

We need to ask ourselves whether there is any point in saving? Isn't money for spending? How can it provide any benefit if it is tucked away in a bank account or invested in stocks, bonds or property trusts? Besides, the things you need are in the here and now. Who knows where you will be in 5, 10 or 15 years, or even whether you will be here at all? You can't take it with you!

These arguments against saving are usually thinly veiled excuses to justify uncontrolled consumption. The justifications to empty your wallet are more likely to be attempts at appeasing your conscience than they are statements of considered thought — and these justifications are flawed anyway. They are based on the premise that to enjoy yourself you need to be consuming. But the surprise for most people is that consumption leads, more often, to exactly the opposite outcome. This is because to spend, you need to earn. And in order to earn, most people need to go to work. While not all people dislike their jobs, most would rather be doing something else. Spending needs to be equated with time spent at work. Time at work for many is not an emotionally fulfilling experience.

The disconnect between spending and work has been rendered even greater by the adoption and widespread use of credit cards and home equity loans. The latter is effectively a super-sized credit card whereby banks allow an extension of credit up to (usually) 80 per cent of the value of your home. Credit cards and home equity loans are too often seen by their holders as extra money rather than what they really are — debt. The holder of a credit card doesn't consider the $10,000 limit as a potential liability rather as $10,000 which is yet to be spent. A home equity loan with a $400,000 cap is seen as an opportunity to buy a new car, extend the home or travel overseas. Indeed, the banks market them along these lines. In reality, it represents the opportunity to incur further burdensome debt with little hope of paying it back unless, of course, the home is ultimately sold. Long after the car has been traded or the holiday has been forgotten, the lasting legacy of hours at work to service the debt is endured.

The best way to bring the disconnect between consumption and work sharply into focus is to equate the price of a potential purchase not with the limit on the credit card, but rather with the time required to earn the purchase price. This is how the calculation should go.

Using your after-tax weekly income (i.e. what actually ends up in your pay cheque), deduct the weekly costs of being at work, including travel (public transport, petrol, motor vehicle running costs, parking), clothing (whatever you have to wear for work), lunches and other expenses. Then calculate the number of hours associated with work. As well as the formal work hours, include time spent travelling to and from work as well as time spent working "out of hours" on nights and weekends. To calculate your hourly rate of pay, divide the adjusted after-tax income by the total weekly hours that work prevents you undertaking other activities. This represents the "true" hourly pay rate. It is often surprising how low this rate actually is.

Now that this rate has been calculated, etch it on your brain. This is the figure you should carry into the shops with you. If that pair of shoes or handbag costs $150, it could well represent 15 hours at work. This is a tangible and realistic way to evaluate the trade-off. Rather than an impulse purchase made with the available credit on your piece of plastic, the real price is based on working hours. How much do you like or dislike going to work? How much do you like that pair of shoes? Are they going to provide enduring useful service or are they going to be worn twice and then pushed to the back of the wardrobe? Is it worth spending 15 hours at work to buy a pair of shoes that will only be worn twice? This approach can be applied to any purchasing decision. When you think this way you are less likely to associate a purchase with the short-lived pleasure resultant from making a spontaneous and unwarranted acquisition, but rather with the more hard-felt need to actually earn the money at the workplace.

Back now to the proposal that you should consume rather than save, and to the arguments that you are "here for a good time and not for a long time" and "you can't take it with you". If you choose to spend every dollar you make as you make it, you will need to "make a dollar" for the rest of your life. Of course, a government funded pension might be available one day but this is meagre at best and might yet be many years away. Saving, however, provides the potential for a self-funded income that will kick in earlier than a pension and also provide for a more comfortable existence when drawn upon.

Those who propose immediate consumption as preferable to the process of saving and investing aren't really thinking beyond the next 10 minutes. They are effectively denying themselves the chance of any form of financial independence and control over their lives. Yet these will be the same individuals who dream of winning the lottery or of extended holidays which will allow them to escape their current circumstances.

They don't see the road from their plight as involving anything as simple as saving. They see relief through earning a higher income or having a one-off cash injection. They are strapped in a financial strait-jacket; they see their saviour to be a cash windfall, an inheritance or a higher remuneration from an as yet to be found job. They continually pass over the real solution, which is to keep more of what they already have.

One of the fundamental principles in medicine is to remove what is known as the aetiology or, in layman's terms, what causes the disease. Attempts to repair damage serve little purpose if the cause of the problem is still present. Why then do people who are financial basket-cases believe their cure excludes removing the cause — the fact that they spend too much? A higher income won't help if their problem is that they spend all the money they earn. Their behaviour is the issue, not the lack of money. This is substance abuse, pure and simple. And, like many substance abusers who deny they have a problem, they too refuse to acknowledge the cause of their problem. They invariably think they just don't have enough money and that everything will be fine when they get more. Giving a chronic spender more money is like managing drug addiction by providing the addict with more heroin.

Let's turn this thinking on its head. If consumption requires hours at work which denies the ability to choose how you spend your time, is it not spending rather than saving that is the act of deprivation? You are depriving yourself of choice. Clearly, this new argument assumes that you would rather be doing something else than working but is this not the case for most? Even those who claim to like their work might be quick to change how they spend their waking hours if they were independently wealthy. The ultimate test as to how much someone really likes their work is to see if they would still be there if attendance was optional.

The reality is that saving should not be associated with deprivation. In fact, it is the most certain road away from deprivation.

Saving will allow the accumulation of capital which, in turn, when invested, will provide a source of passive income. Passive income doesn't require the trading of time or effort for its receipt. Typically, passive income takes the form of interest, rental or dividends from investments. Moderate amounts allow a reduction in working hours, while significant amounts allow you to decide whether you even need to work at all.

To achieve this not all money that is earned is consumed. Rather a proportion is saved and invested. This fundamental difference in thinking separates the wealthy from the poor. Researchers Steven Venti and David Wise found that it was saving, not the size of income that provided the greatest assurance of wealth accumulation.[8] They found that at all levels of lifetime earnings there was a wide dispersion in the accumulated wealth of families approaching retirement. Interestingly, a significant proportion of high income families saved little and low income families could save a great deal. They found that the bulk of the dispersion in wealth was attributable to differences in the amounts that households chose to save and that a high income was no guarantee of high net worth.

This might sound surprising, but it shouldn't. The surest way to accumulate wealth is to save part of what is earned and to invest it. Without saving it doesn't matter whether you earn $30,000 per year or $3 million per year. You will end up in the same position — broke.

The answer to the question "Why save at all?" can be stated simply as "to achieve financial independence". Saving provides the fuel for investment. Without saving you are reliant on borrowings for investment which then introduces further risk and a reliance on capital gain as the principal source of return. The surest way to financial independence is to save and to invest. The two are interdependent. Without saving there is no fuel for investment and without investment the savings cannot grow. Why then do people deny this reality? And why are many of those who are able to accept its simple truth still incapable of saving?

You will discover the answer to these questions and gain a greater understanding of achieving financial security as you read further in the book.

CHAPTER 6

Why don't we save?

*"My problem lies in reconciling my gross habits
with my net income."*

ERROL FLYNN

*"Life is not long enough; human nature desires quick
results, there is a peculiar zest in making money quickly,
and remoter gains are discounted by the average
man at a very high rate."*

JOHN MAYNARD KEYNES

The psychology associated with the act of saving is complex. There are many emotional forces working against it. Sure, deep down we tell ourselves that we should save, just as we know that we should exercise and eat green vegetables. But that's not to say it's going to happen. This chapter and the next explore the reasons why we fail to save.

As a starting point few people actually go through the process of calculating how much they could amass if they undertook a savings programme. Even if they did, they might then be deterred by the time it takes to accrue a material benefit. Faced with the opportunity to consume now, little regard is likely to be given to saving over a period of one year let alone 10 or 15.

Perpetually working against the saving process is the ever-present temptation of immediate consumption. We are reminded of what others have and we don't. We are offered credit, lay-by and interest-free terms. We are constantly being exposed to advertising and the conscious (and sometimes sub-conscious) messages that prey on our socially moulded desire to conform to our peers' materialistic achievements and expectations. The ability to buy goods now and to pay for them later has never been easier and the fact that most of us behave this way means that going into debt carries a lesser social stigma than it used to. In fact, debt fuelled consumption is considered to constitute normal behaviour and therefore has social acceptance.

As strange as it may sound, there is a social stigma attached to saving. The word "frugal" once was associated with social responsibility, but now is synonymous with "cheap", "tight", "skinflint" and "tightwad". Perversely, excessive consumption carries social kudos. Those who blow their pay cheque on "having a good time" are revered. They indulge in "retail therapy" or show disregard for tomorrow by spending all their money today. And often driving this free spending is the desire to avoid being ridiculed. To avoid detrimental names and tags we resist activities which will attract them. Socialisation is a powerful force. Even though we like to think that we are not influenced by the thoughts and opinions of others in reality we usually are.

Saving is often associated with budgeting. For some, budgeting conjures up images of a pencil and notepad, counting pennies, constantly chasing the lowest priced goods and restricting purchases to the bare necessities of life. Although the fanatical budgeter might behave this way, budgeting is not necessarily a process of perpetual price tracking or purchase limiting. It need only be undertaken occasionally — as little as once or twice a year — in order to get a handle on where the money is actually going. Budgeting should be a process that periodically raises awareness, allows checks, controls and limits on what might otherwise be an unfettered disposal of every cent you earn. Besides, budgeting can be a soft process, one that places boundaries rather than the imposition of strict and constant sanctions on your life. Budgets take in many other factors, including current lifestyle, future financial ambitions and a genuine consideration of what you really value in life.

Saving is often seen as too pedestrian. Most people want money now! They want quick results. They can't provide their own solution to their dilemma but they don't see how saving can be the answer. The irony is that, linked to investment, saving is the most certain means of reaching financial independence. Saving should not be seen solely as the process of accumulating enough money for an annual holiday or a plasma TV. Saving should be a consistent, regular process linked to the investment process. Over time, these two combined activities can produce powerful results.

Unfortunately, few people connect the process of saving small amounts and investing over an extended period with the accumulation of significant wealth. Yet simply saving $5 per day and investing the accumulated amount once a year will result in the accumulation of in excess of $200,000 after a 30 year period at a return of 8 per cent. Saving $25 per day will make you a millionaire. Unfortunately for most, they can't wait this long. They want a tangible asset they can show to the world right now as evidence of their financial and investing acumen.

Many people want to invest but have no money. What to do? In an economic analogy to having their cake and eating it too, they deny the need to save for investment and approach the bank for an "investment loan". This might involve funding a stock portfolio or, more commonly, a rental property. It doesn't appear to matter to them that the asset they just bought has an equivalent debt liability attached to it. The fact that their real net worth still remains at zero immediately after the asset purchase doesn't seem to cross their mind. Any thought of this, if undertaken at all, is far outweighed by the sense of acquiring the asset, of putting it into the "portfolio", of putting their name to it.

Many confuse investing with doing a deal. They think they are investing only when some form of activity takes place. They feel the need to be buying or selling. But the reality is that for most this activity is counter-productive. Not everyone is a successful deal maker. The real investor acquires high-yielding assets and holds them for long periods rather than trading them. They are conspicuous by their inactivity.

Additionally, there is a powerful force that works against the process of borrowing to invest. The need to service the resultant debt soaks up the cash flow the asset would otherwise provide in the form of ongoing dividend or rental income. The investor therefore becomes reliant upon capital gain as the principal, if not the sole source of investment return. Faced one day with the realisation that the debt used to finance the asset has to be paid back might necessitate the forced liquidation of the asset. Following the payment of transaction costs, non-indexed capital gains tax and years of negative income returns, it does indeed need to be a significant capital gain to provide a rate of return that warrants the whole exercise. As a further consideration the financial landscape is littered with "investors" who were forced to sell assets that actually dropped in price. Whilst this often affects those who buy stock on margin the use of debt to purchase real estate can produce the same result. By way of example it was the deflation of a worldwide property bubble in 2007-2008 which brought international economies and financial markets to their knees.

Most investors who borrow to invest are unlikely to calculate whether the exercise is warranted. They may feel "wealthy" for a period because they have control of an asset. The novice investor may justify his behaviour by focusing on the difference between the purchase price and the sale price with no regard to inflation, the time value of money and the leakage of transaction costs, land taxes, capital gains taxes, maintenance costs and the years of negative income returns. Like the gambler who only tells you of his wins the judgment is quick and simple: "I sold it for more than I paid for it".

Investors who buy assets with borrowed money, whether that asset is in the form of stock or property, often become singularly obsessed with capital gain. They trivialise or ignore the power of reinvestment of income. They may tend to do this because, in servicing the debt from the income stream, little or no free income is available. But it is also likely that many fail to realise how significant reinvestment of income is in contributing to overall returns. Reinvestment of income can also be described as the compounding of returns. The investor who places no importance on the reinvestment of returns and in many cases even accepts a negative return in exchange for a tax credit, misses out on what Albert Einstein described as:

"The greatest mathematical discovery of all time".

Einstein was referring to the power of compound interest, of which the reinvestment of investment returns is a practical example.

Saving combined with investment negates the need to borrow. This then allows the power of income reinvestment to deliver enhanced investment returns. It removes the risk of increasing interest costs eroding overall returns. Finally it bestows control over the underlying asset, denying the possibility of a forced sale under the weight of onerous loan covenants during a period of depressed asset prices.

If you want to kill the perception that saving to invest is pedestrian in nature then all you need to do is to rediscover the compound interest formula. Sit down with a calculator or personal computer and model various combinations of saving, time and return. It will be an eye-opening exercise.

CHAPTER 7

Keeping up with the Joneses

"Too many people spend money they haven't earned to buy things they don't want to impress people they don't like."

WILL ROGERS

Two powerful reasons why people don't save can be explained by the two "Ss" which I will discuss throughout this chapter. People work for a number of reasons. Clearly the establishment of a sense of identity is one reason. A profession is commonly linked to standing in the community. This standing comes from either the intrinsic worth that work provides to the community or, in our society, an inferred standing if that particular industry or profession is highly paid. One commonly asked question when people first meet is: "What do you do for a living?" This helps the enquirer to pigeon-hole the enquiree within a social, intellectual or financial group.

Putting identity aside, what are further motives of the worker in seeking employment? It enables basic needs to be fulfilled — food, shelter and clothing. If defined simply, these three needs can be satisfied on a very basic wage. But the definition of "need" varies, depending on who is asked the question. The term "need" is more often interpreted as the expectation of a certain "standard of living". In turn, "standard of living" can mean different things to different socio-economic groups. It also varies through time as general material affluence increases in line with increases in economic productivity.

Each succeeding generation demands more to satisfy its basic expectations of "need". Consumption has developed into something that is more than a provision of physiological needs. Rather it is used as a badge of status, as an expression of financial standing. Driving this is man's innate desire to be accepted. And to succeed is to be accepted.

Previously the material benchmarks used for establishing social acceptance have been defined by observing friends, relatives and neighbours. However, with the development of broad-based media through television and the internet, the family next door is less likely to be the benchmark by which material expectations are set. Now, sports stars, entertainers and businessmen are increasingly being lavished with incomes that were unheard of only a generation ago. These people have become the new benchmarks, the new "Joneses", the new "standard of living". The problem is that people with incomes that are only a fraction of these conspicuous consumers are trying to emulate them. They see themselves to be ever short of money. There is an epidemic of people in the wealthiest nations who feel they don't have enough; that they need more.

The two most insidious forces working against our ability to save have social origins. Largely inconspicuous but with enormous effect, they are so deeply embedded in our psyche that most people don't even know they exist, let alone appreciate their power.

These two erosive forces are (1) sociology and (2) status. Efforts to save are more often than not foiled as people spend every available dollar in a game of material "keeping up with the Joneses".

Integral to this behaviour is that man has a deep-seated need to be accepted by those around him. Strangely, this acceptance doesn't even need to be from someone he knows. The status-seeker will gain an inner glow equally from the comments of a stranger as he would from a family member or friend. A material object such as a car, house or article of clothing often is bought in the hope of making others envious. Therefore it is not the object itself which is sought but, rather, social acceptance from others.

The power of ridicule should never be underestimated in the shaping of purchasing decisions. Indeed, ridicule and public humiliation have been used as a form of punishment. In order to avoid it, people dress, behave and conform to general expectations afraid that if they don't they will incite such comments as "I would never be seen dead wearing such and such" or "doesn't he realise that no-one does that anymore?" Far safer to err on the side of conformity. These emotions form the very backbone of the clothing and fashion industry.

So how does this relate to saving? In our attempts to conform we mimic our peers. Our peers might be our friends, neighbours, relatives or those we would like to have as peers — those in the media, on television and in magazines. How they conduct their lives, the houses they live in, the cars they drive and their holiday destinations all set a benchmark which consciously or unconsciously we seek to emulate. What matters is whether an individual has less or more than those around him. Since he is more concerned by what someone thinks, an actual level of material prosperity is not fixed. It can vary through time and geography. It doesn't matter to an American that he has significantly more than the average Tanzanian, nor does he care that his house is twice the size of his grandparents'. He is more likely to be concerned by how it compares to those of his current social peers. It doesn't matter that his grandfather used to catch public transport, rather the fact that his friend's BMW is newer than his own.

This behaviour can have a profound effect on your ability to save. If there is a growing trend for people to take out large mortgages to buy homes and to finance the purchase of European cars through lease arrangements, then there will be a tendency for others to follow suit. To risk ridicule by driving an old car or having shabby furniture becomes socially unacceptable. And if others are funding their purchases with debt, then surely it must be acceptable to do the same? The notion of saving for some future benefit is easily discarded when there is a pressing need for immediate status-driven consumption.

While there is a tendency for people to deny that they behave in this manner, the reality is that they do. Inputs often require little cognitive manipulation before they are interpreted as needs even if in reality they clearly aren't. The danger is that if you behave like everyone else, you will become like everyone else — perpetually broke.

Observations of this type of behaviour are not recent. The book *Democracy in America* written by nineteenth century French political philosopher and sociologist Alexis de Tocqueville was an early work of social comment which addressed this subject[9]. In 1831, de Tocqueville, at the age of 26, travelled to America with the aim of studying what he called "the future shape and temperament of the world". At this time it was only 55 years since the United States had declared itself independent of English rule, but already it had started the process of taking on its own economic identity, fuelled by an abundance of "wealth bestowing" natural resources.

Although de Tocqueville travelled to America at a time when most of the civilised world could be referred to as an aristocracy, he recognised that the rapid growth of the new American democracy was more representative of what the world could expect in the future. As a democracy, America acknowledged an individual's place in society was not defined by the class into which he or she was born. America from the outset aimed to establish a classless society. This was spelt out in 1776 within its Declaration of Independence which stated that "all men are created equal". In reality, however, rather than establishing a democracy, America has developed towards a meritocratic society. Rather than a society in which everyone is equal, America provides material rewards more closely linked to the effort and merit of individuals. Many countries have followed this model.

What struck de Tocqueville in 1831 was that the abolition of the old class structure had resulted in there being no upper limit on material expectations. In the nine months that he stayed in America he observed that despite Americans enjoying a standard of living higher than that of his native France, they appeared to be dissatisfied with their affluence and wanted more. Despite de Tocqueville's observations having been made almost 200 years ago, they are as relevant today as they were then.

In line with people's desire for more, economic prosperity has delivered more — but there seems to be no end to human desire.

There has been an ever-increasing flow of material goods over the last few hundred years stemming from the productivity gains achieved during the Industrial and Information Revolutions. But despite the exponential growth in the goods and services available since de Tocqueville made his observations, people continue to be dissatisfied. Although the Declaration of Independence insists that all men are created equal, most don't wish to be seen as equal. Individuals continue to seek superiority over their fellow man in one form or another.

The vehicle used for establishing this differentiation in "status" has changed over time, and no doubt will continue to change. In our current society material symbols are used to bestow status. The phrase "status symbol", is attributed to Norwegian-American sociologist and economist, Thorstein Veblen. In his book *The Theory of the Leisure Class* Veblen provided commentary on the social attitudes and values existing in America in the late nineteenth century.[10] He saw society's resources being wasted by those who had the greatest access to them, and questioned the values that condoned the misuse of wealth.

Of course, there are many ways that status can be sought, and not all are based on the purchase of material symbols. At a golf club, the member with the lowest handicap is likely to be held in high regard. Alternatively, physical appearance, strength or oratory skills are all qualities which can bestow status. But within the society described by Veblen, one pervasive measure is symbolic material wealth. Many regard this as the holy grail. But clearly by its definition alone, it is impossible for superiority to be achieved by all. Faced with the reality that most fall short, others feign wealth through buying symbols, often with borrowed money, to give the appearance of success.

Combining the observations of de Tocqueville and Veblen helps explain why so many people are dissatisfied. People don't crave the object but, rather, the attention and acceptance that possessing the object bestows. If it bestows attention and acceptance then that object is sought. What de Tocqueville and Veblen were observing is that it is not enough to own what others own. People want to own more objects and objects of a higher quality in order to be differentiated, to be accepted and admired. That is, to achieve status.

As the general level of material wealth within a society rises, so the bar is raised forever higher and it becomes necessary to seek ever greater levels of materialism for that differentiation to be established.

It is still possible today to make the same social observations as those made by Veblen in the late nineteenth century. Why would someone drive a $400,000 Ferrari, capable of reaching 250km per hour in order to travel to the local shops? Why not for any other reason than to be noticed? Why would childless couples or those with small families build monstrous sized homes containing movie theatres and underground garages capable of housing several cars other than to declare to the world that they have the financial capacity to do so?

American born psychologist Abraham Maslow proposed in his 1943 paper "A Theory of Human Motivation" that humans seek to satisfy a progressively higher set of needs.[11] These needs occupy a hierarchy and as each need or set of needs is met the individual seeks to fulfil the needs of the next level. Maslow's hierarchy of needs is often depicted as a pyramid consisting of five levels. The lowest level is represented by physiological needs. An individual deprived of food, water or shelter will seek these before anything else but once obtained they are taken for granted. The individual will then seek the next level of unfulfilled needs, represented by security and health. Higher levels consist of belonging, self-esteem and self-actualisation. Self-esteem and respect by others come fairly high up the pyramid and it is at this level that most people in developed societies are operating. The lower levels of food, water and shelter have well and truly been taken care of for most.

In keeping with people's motivation, their principal reason for buying status symbols is to gain attention and fulfil the emotional needs of belonging and acceptance.

American psychologist and philosopher, William James suggested that self-esteem is significantly influenced by the esteem in which others hold us. Self-observation would see us agreeing with James. We have all experienced a feeling of pleasure when acknowledged or complimented even if the person paying the compliment is unknown to us. Yet there is a dark side to James' description of self-esteem. He describes it as being directly related to our success, but inversely related to our expectations. Or put in mathematical terms, self-esteem is measured by using our success as the numerator and our expectations as the denominator.

$$\text{Self-esteem} \quad = \quad \frac{\text{Success}}{\text{Expectations}}$$

Therefore, as our expectations rise in the face of a static level of success, so our self-esteem falls, all other things being equal.

Be aware that these expectations are moulded by a mix of internal and external forces. While we experience them ourselves, they develop from our attempts to stay ahead of the pack in terms of materially-judged supremacy. If these values are the ones by which the individual wants to be judged, then in order to maintain an acceptable level of self-esteem he finds it unacceptable to lower his expectations (the denominator) and therefore seeks ever increasing levels of success (read materialism). Or putting it another way, there is the potential for frustration to become the prevailing emotion. The goal will be forever pushed out of reach. And, unlike the pursuit of worthwhile goals that provide a sense of meaning, this is unlikely to be felt when the goal being pursued consists of a perpetual string of material acquisitions and disposals.

What is particularly disconcerting is that the list of items which are seen to carry status is growing. There was a time when these items were limited to houses, motor vehicles, clothing and jewellery. But we now are talking about utilitarian objects like pens, watches, cooking appliances, bicycles and sunglasses. Naomi Klein, in her book *No Logo*, identified a trend of corporations spending seemingly endless dollars on advertising in order to create a desired name or brand.[12] This is then conspicuously applied to a wide range of low cost items which are subsequently sold at inflated prices to a brand-hungry public for significant profit. People therefore don't spend $10 on a plain T-shirt, rather, they spend four to five times that amount to buy one with a "designer" name splashed across the front. This practice is insidiously creeping into everyday purchasing decisions. The irony is that in the attempt to create the illusion of being materially wealthy, people are actually preventing themselves from ever getting there.

Throw into this mix the debt factor. A lack of money doesn't stop anyone spending. Friends, relatives and neighbours are unlikely to examine your bank statements but they will notice your new car. People try to justify debt-funded purchasing decisions as life enriching but the reality is that they usually have a detrimental impact on how life pans out. The object bought to impress soon becomes old, common or unfashionable. It is rarely bought solely for its utility. So, when the item is no longer a focus of attention or approval, it becomes useless. Yet when the owner disposes of it, he usually finds no one else wants it either. At best, if a buyer is found, it is sold at a much lower price than for which it was originally bought. Something else is then needed to fill the void and so the cycle continues. Let me introduce you to the modern consumer.

So how does all of this relate to a discussion on saving? The most powerful point to be made is that the successful saver needs to be aware of these emotions. Faced with a direct question, many people would say that this behaviour does not apply to them, but they would be fooling themselves. Admittedly, the degree to which this affects different people varies but there is a need to acknowledge its existence at some level since it can be extremely counterproductive to the saving process. To assist in your rejection of this behaviour, remember that those people who are really important to you, that is close family and real friends, don't judge you by what you own.

And as for the attention of strangers, you would be better placed to consider the words of nineteenth century philosopher Arthur Schopenhauer who said:

"We will gradually become indifferent to what goes on in the minds of other people when we acquire an adequate knowledge of the superficial nature of their thoughts, of the narrowness of their views and the number of their errors. Whoever attaches a lot of value to the opinions of others pays them too much honour."[13]

Applying this to the saving and investment process, a very clear concept can be established. Don't buy just to acquire symbols of status as most of these tend to be overpriced and serve their purpose for only a short time. More importantly, the purpose they do serve should seriously be questioned. An even greater financial crime is to borrow in order to buy these items.

And if, after all this consideration, you are still influenced by how people see you, then consider this. The ability to live an independent life through the establishment of a source of income that you don't need to work for will impress those around you much more than the fleeting attention you will receive from undertaking a long string of consumer purchases that are subsequently relegated to used car yards, opportunity shops and land fill.

CHAPTER 8

The Industrial Revolution and the Stationary State

I saw a man pursuing the horizon
Round and round they sped
I was disturbed at this
I accosted the man
"It is futile", I said
"You can never …"
"You lie", he cried and ran on.

STEVEN CRANE

Most of us move blindly through life. We behave and act within a cocoon of perceptions moulded by our social environment. We adopt the values of others and call them our own. We don't question these values, so when challenged we defend our stance, not from a base of deep consideration but from the benchmark set by common belief. In doing this we guarantee our inability to achieve anything other than what those around us achieve.

How do you go about tempering the emotional forces of compliance with social norm and of status seeking behaviour? Clearly the first thing to do is to be aware of them. Hopefully a rational individual will recognise their futility. Throughout history great minds have recognised this and have voiced social comment. But as is the case of visionaries who perceive a problem that others don't, their words have gone largely unheeded by the masses.

The following outlines the thoughts of some of these visionaries, their comments and beliefs. The voices have become louder since the start of the Industrial Revolution.

In 1698, an Englishman, Thomas Savery, patented an early steam engine. An intended application of Savery's steam engine was to pump water from coal mines, but its design was flawed as it proved to be both unreliable and incapable of raising water from depth. The first steam engine capable of performing the task adequately was attributed to Thomas Newcomen in 1712. Many identify this event as the dawn of the Industrial Age.

Previously, economic evolution had been slow. Human needs for thousands of years had been met from basic farming and cottage-based production. Before steam, power had come from wind, flowing water, beasts of burden and man's own sweat and toil. Production techniques were labour intensive and often limited to the skill and speed of individual workers. But with the development of steam power manual labour was increasingly replaced by machines.

This resulted in an enormous increase in man's ability to transform raw materials into items of consumption. For those countries bountiful in ingenuity, natural resources, carbon-based fossil fuels and a willing workforce, the economic rewards came quickly. There were significant boosts in the standard of living for those living in these countries. Increased economic production led to advances in infrastructure, housing, education, nutrition and health. But once improvements in these basic needs had been met, what then? There was still potential for further productivity gains, so how should these be utilised? Once the basic needs of a country's population had been met, further productivity gains offered three potential outcomes. Firstly, the increased production achieved by countries rich in natural resources could have been distributed to countries with less. The development of improved housing, sanitation, education and agriculture could have been universally provided. Alternatively, there was the opportunity for those in wealthy countries to simply maintain their existing levels of consumption but with less effort devoted to production. Increases in productivity provided the opportunity for significant reductions in individual working hours but with no alteration to economic wellbeing. Or thirdly, working hours could have been maintained with the increased levels of production allowing for ever-increasing levels of consumption. Clearly it is the third option which has been chosen. Productivity gains have been taken as the opportunity to consume more.

It has long been recognised that improvements in the efficiency of production have offered the opportunity for a reduction in the hours spent at work with no decline in levels of economic wellbeing. One early commentator and critic was the brilliant and perceptive nineteenth century British economist John Stuart Mill. He felt that the production increases from the Industrial Revolution were being misused. Mill's two-volume book *Principles of Political Economy* might run to more than 1000 pages but it is the short seven-page chapter entitled "Of the Stationary State" which provides the most powerful social comment. Mill questions why human achievement was increasingly being judged by material measures. He felt better measures could be used; that material development beyond what was an already acceptable level was unnecessary, even counterproductive. He wrote:

> "It is scarcely necessary to remark that a stationary condition of capital and population implies no stationary state of human improvement. There would be as much scope as ever for all kinds of mental culture, and moral and social progress; as much room for improving the Art of Living, and much more likelihood of its being improved, when minds ceased to be engrossed by the art of getting on."[14]

Remember that this was written a century and a half ago.

In keeping with Mill's concept of the Stationary State, John Maynard Keynes, one of the most influential economists of the twentieth century, suggested in 1930, that economic growth provided the potential for a 15-hour working week.[15] Applying

Keynes' suggested economic growth rate of 2% that could have been achieved by 1980. Best described as an opportunity lost, working hours have actually increased over this period. Also, women have increasingly entered the workforce over the same time. But why have Mill's words been ignored and why have Keynes' predictions failed to eventuate? Why have increasing levels of productivity failed to result in a decrease in hours spent at work? The answer is that the opportunity to produce more has been embraced as the opportunity to consume more. Status and attempts at differentiation by accumulating more objects of fashion have seen a spiral of consumption way beyond the realms of necessity. The bar which represents social norm has been continually rising so that ever-increasing levels of consumption are necessary to clear it.

Mill observed and described the same behaviour in his time:

"I know not why it should be a matter of congratulation that persons who are already richer than anyone needs to be, should have doubled their means of consuming things which give little or no pleasure except as representative of wealth ... It is only in the backward countries of the world that increased production is still an important object."[16]

Long before Mill's words warning of the futility of excessive consumption, others had voiced the same sentiments. Almost 2000 years ago in the town of Oinoandra, in the south-west of what we now know as Turkey, there lived a wealthy man named Diogenes. In about 120 AD Diogenes had erected a substantial wall in the town's marketplace on which were inscribed the thoughts of the Greek philosopher Epicurus. Epicurus had lived four centuries before Diogenes but his teachings and philosophies, particularly on the subject of what brought balance to human life, were so powerful that they had been passed on through the generations. Diogenes had inscribed onto the face of the marketplace wall the following Epicurean thoughts which were clearly aimed at the activity of the shoppers below:

"Luxurious food and drinks ... in no way produce freedom from harm and a healthy condition in the flesh.

"One must regard wealth beyond what is natural as of no more use than water to a container that is full to overflowing. Real value is not generated by theatres and baths and perfumes and ointments ... but by natural science."[17]

Despite the fundamental sense of Epicurus' and Mill's words, people and governments of today speak and behave in a totally contrary fashion. For example, it is disconcerting to observe the response of governments around the world following the collapse of financial markets in 2008 and 2009. Following the fallout from the Sub-prime Crisis economies around the world came to a grinding halt. The catalyst for the crisis was the collapse of a housing bubble which had developed in a number of industrialised countries, but particularly the US. This resulted in a near cessation of the excessive debt-funded consumption which had been fuelled by the generally ill conceived perception by many that inflated house prices had somehow enhanced their personal wealth. When it was realised that the party was over stock markets plummeted, unemployment rose and businesses and institutions with high levels of debt fell over like dominoes.

How did governments respond to the crisis? By putting more money into the hands of its citizens through broad based cash handouts. People were encouraged to spend as quickly and freely as possible on anything they chose. And where would much of these purchased items end up? More land fill. The crisis was caused by the multitude living beyond their means. The solution? To spend more. Consumption of anything useless, disposable or shiny in order to keep people busy producing objects that were useless, disposable and shiny. Sure, it does make sense for governments to spend when the private sector isn't. This will help to keep employment alive so minimising the hardship of job losses with its associated personal suffering. But why not spend the money on things that provide a lasting benefit to the community like schools, hospitals and infrastructure projects? The politicians will respond to this question by saying that they want to pump money into the economy within a short time frame. But the reality is that the resultant expenditure achieves little by way of lasting benefit and is more likely a sop to their political popularity. When sitting there watching your government funded TV you are likely to remember where it came from.

The greatest hardship during an economic downturn is borne by those who become unemployed. Another way of avoiding the problem of increasing levels of unemployment has been stated by men who are wiser than most of today's politicians. Spread the workload of those who are fully employed with those who face imminent job loss. Therefore there would be work for all but for fewer hours.

America's cry for increased consumption as a solution to its economic woes is a short term fix. In some ways it's like curing unemployment by handing out shovels to the unemployed and directing half of them to dig holes and the other half to fill them in again. But unlike digging and filling in holes, which is a futile but relatively harmless exercise, the production and disposal of an excessive volume of goods is not harmless. It is depleting the world's natural resources at a disconcerting rate.

The thinking of our politicians and economists is strongly influenced by their preoccupation with the use of production based national accounts. One commonly used measure, inflation adjusted GDP, is used to compare economic production between periods of time in order to assess whether a country's economy is growing or declining. GDP per capita is also utilised for international comparison. As discussed in chapter 4, "League tables" are constructed, allowing a country to compare its economic prosperity with other countries. However, it has been argued repeatedly that such a figure does not provide a true indication of a country's overall prosperity. Included in the calculation are numerous activities which are poor indicators of wellbeing. Some actually indicate the opposite. Also, there are many factors which are overlooked but should be included since they are better indicators of true wellbeing. Their exclusion is most likely associated with the difficulty in measuring and quantifying them.

Factors which could be ascribed to defining a country's wellbeing, but which aren't considered in the economists' and politicians' analysis, are political freedom, air and water quality, climate and the state of emotional and physical health of its residents. It also could be argued that some factors which are included in the calculation of GDP, such as expenditure on pollution control, weapon production and expenditure on repair and replacement following war or natural disaster, should not be included in a measure used to judge a country's wellbeing. This fact was recognised from the day these measures were first devised.

John Maynard Keynes, John Hicks and Simon Kuznets first developed the concepts of national accounting which economists, politicians and the financial markets so avidly follow today. Yet the originators of these economic measures stressed their limitations and repeatedly warned against their use as indicators of national prosperity. Kuznets said in 1934: "The welfare of a nation can scarcely be inferred from a measurement of national income ..."

He made the following statement in 1962:

"Distinctions must be kept in mind between quantity and quality of growth, between its costs and returns, and between the short and long run ... Goals for 'more' growth should specify more growth of what and for what."

Kuznets' words echo those of John Stuart Mill 100 years earlier. And what of the world since Mill 150 years ago and Kuznets 50 years ago? Not only have their words been largely ignored but it seems that the need to acknowledge them has become increasingly relevant. Mill, in his writings on the Stationary State, intermingled his comments on national economic behaviour with those of individual behaviour. Clearly this makes sense since his words are as applicable to the individual as they are to a nation as a whole. An individual can practise the behaviour described as the Stationary State. This is extremely important because, if you feel frustrated by the futility of the behaviour of those around you, then you can take matters into your own hands. If you feel that most people are not capitalising on productivity gains which could otherwise allow a reduction in working hours, then you have the opportunity to take action yourself. But you need to disconnect what you see as important from what society sees as important — particularly at a consumption level.

If you accept a particular level of material wealth and stop seeking a higher one, you are practising Stationary State. As you seek to improve your life through other means such as religious, interpersonal, educational or emotional improvement without emphasis on a financial state, then you are practising Stationary State. Pursuit of unbounded materialism would then appear to be as futile to the individual as one-dimensional economic growth would be to a nation.

Whilst Mill's book primarily addressed economic principles, it was intertwined with social philosophy such as the following:

"I confess I am not charmed with the idea of life held out by those who think that the normal state of human beings is that of struggling to get on; that the trampling, crushing, elbowing, and treading on each other's heels, which form the existing type of social life, are the most desirable lot of human kind, or anything but the disagreeable symptoms of one of the phases of industrial progress."[18]

Since Mill penned those words many economists have expressed similar sentiments. Australian economist Clive Hamilton recently expressed his concern that this behaviour, if continued, would have an irreversible deleterious impact on the ecology of our planet.[19] The number of voices joining this chorus of sentiment is increasing every year. Clearly the degradation of our planet is a high price to pay for what essentially boils down to selfish and misdirected social behaviour.

If Mill's concept of the Stationary State had been accepted we would all now be working fewer hours. Would our quality of life be less? If measured on a consumption basis — yes. But by all other measures it would most likely have improved.

Let's hypothesise for a while. As judged in 1930, Keynes felt that the working week could be reduced from 40 hours to 15 possibly within a 50 year period. Let's assume the same argument had applied to the 50 years just past. This would take us back to the era of rock 'n' roll, an era of boundless optimism as depicted by the television show "Happy Days". People of the '50s and '60s never gave a microsecond's thought to owning a mobile phone, a plasma surround sound entertainment system, a five-car garage beneath a 50 square home, a turbo powered European four-wheel drive car or any of the other material items that some people believe today are essential to living a fulfilled life.

Yet people living in the US in the '50s saw themselves as affluent. Indeed, in 1958, economist John Kenneth Galbraith described the United States as "the affluent society".

Logic would indicate that there was no need to seek further "affluence" from that time. In 1958 people in the United States were already affluent. But unfortunately, logic doesn't seem to count since it has repeatedly been shown that securing increased levels of affluence fails to resolve man's economic desires. History profoundly shows this to be the case. The wonderful twist here is that if you have the independence of mind to step off the materialism treadmill, you can achieve the benefits described by Mill and Keynes, independent of whether the nation as a whole chooses to or not.

To practise Stationary State on an individual basis, to ignore the social norm of ever increasing levels of material consumption is an extremely difficult step for most of us to take. Defiance of social convention does not come easily. However, for those who can, two very powerful opportunities present themselves.

Firstly, if consumption is lowered then greater levels of saving are achievable. Higher levels of saving lead to enhanced capital accumulation as this money is invested. The sooner a body of capital is established, the earlier a passive income flows from that capital. Hence, the earlier you can have the freedom to live life as you choose.

Secondly, if consumption expectations are lowered, then the size of the passive income stream which you demand to maintain an acceptable quality of life is also lowered. Since less income is demanded less capital needs to be accumulated to provide it. Combine these two facts and you can see that there is a double effect: a faster rate of capital accumulation chasing a smaller target. By lowering consumption levels there now is a much greater chance that the capital target will be reached.

If life is spent pursuing ever-increasing consumption levels then a sufficient body of capital will never be accumulated. Potential savings will be perpetually misdirected towards both immediate consumption and the servicing of debt resultant from yesterday's consumption. By trimming expenditure, living within set financial means and investing the surplus then some very powerful financial forces are unleashed.

CHAPTER 9

Income amnesia

"Luxuries, once tasted, tend to be regarded as necessities."

MICHAEL LE BOEUF

For the reader who has lived beyond early adulthood, cast your mind back to school days and those immediately beyond adolescence. During that period it is likely that little was owned, at most an old car. Spare time was spent principally with friends. Pastimes such as "hanging out", parties, camping, surfing and a variety of other leisure activities filled the time which wasn't taken up by work or study. There was little, if any, money in the bank. The focus was on enjoyment rather than "getting on". There was travel or adventure and activities such as skiing, trekking and sailing took precedence. Since spare time was largely spent with friends, laughter and good times were the norm. Life was usually carefree and uncomplicated. Enjoyment didn't require a large pay cheque as activities usually involved social interaction with others rather than attempts to impress materially. Many people who have passed through this stage of their life could ask themselves why is it that their lives are now so different?

These ingredients of a good life are, for many, forgotten or discarded. Why have so many middle-aged people forgotten how to enjoy themselves? Somehow they became caught up in something that swept them away to another place. How is it that they used to live happily on a token income yet now need at least six figures just to pay the bills? Certainly taking on family responsibilities accounts for a large part of this but it doesn't provide the total answer. The answer also lies in the process of socialisation. As life progresses it is the social expectation that more things are accumulated. Each of us becomes consciously or unconsciously drawn into the process.

This process is closely associated with another best referred to as "income amnesia". In explaining it, consider employees who are living on low incomes. Most exist reasonably well as long as debt doesn't become a predominant factor in their lives. The bills are paid, a car is run and there is enough for food, housing and clothing. This state of affairs should be expected if employed and living in a wealthy industrialised country such as Australia or the United States. The worker might, on the whole, be relatively satisfied with his lot, although there often is an underlying feeling that a little more would help. In the absence of any saving there is usually no perception as to where the money has gone and no analysis of present or past spending habits. This could well explain the behaviour of millions of people in industrialised societies.

Consider then that a pay rise is awarded to our worker. The extra money is paid into the worker's bank account by his employer and is therefore added to the general pool of money available for consumption. This money is spent as well. If an extra $50 per week is awarded it is a near certainty that there won't be $2,600 in the worker's bank account one year later.

Assume now that over the next several years our worker starts to climb, by way of promotion, up the corporate ladder and that with each promotion there is a commensurate increase in salary. But usually with each pay increase there are new ways found to dispose of the newly derived income. A mobile phone is bought, a better car, new and more expensive clothes, holidays to more exotic destinations, $50 bottles of wine instead of cheaper offerings. The list is virtually endless. With every pay rise discretionary spending is increased to match it. Still there are no savings. The bank account is cleared as regularly as the pay is deposited. The process has evolved over time so the worker has not really been conscious of it occurring. Ask if the income which he received several years ago is enough to support current "needs" and you are likely to be answered with a very definite "no". In fact, he might say, and believe with absolute conviction, that no one could live on such a meagre income as he once earned. He has become accustomed to a new set of values. Interestingly, it is unlikely that he has even been aware of the shift.

In order to counteract this phenomenon consider the act of "paying yourself first". It is a great way of saving, particularly for those lacking financial self-discipline. Pay yourself first means that any new money resulting from a pay rise is automatically diverted into a designated bank account, an account not utilised for anything except accumulating savings. Pay yourself first acknowledges that if the money is never seen it cannot be missed. This is easy in today's electronic age. Internet banking allows the establishment of a system of automatic money transfer between accounts. By using this technique the transfer occurs automatically in a regular, reliable manner. Since the cash is never actually seen it is out of temptation's way. The only self-discipline required is the understanding that the money is not to be spent. It must not be withdrawn from the account in order to finance items like a holiday or a new car. It must be dedicated to the process of capital accumulation. It must be thought of as providing funds for the purpose of investment.

Establishing a flow of funds into a savings account through the system of pay yourself first need not be limited solely to pay increases. The process can also be used to capture a proportion of existing salary that is currently being spent. By allocating a proportion of your salary to a separate account money can then accumulate out of harm's way.

Essential to the process of paying yourself first is the fundamental acceptance of the concept "more is not better". It doesn't require adoption of extreme austerity but it does require an acknowledge-ment and adoption of the general philosophy that there is benefit in tempering excessive consumption. It is important to stress that this does not mean deprivation. Life can be spent well without spending all that you earn. In considering this further it is interesting to look at various groups through history who have voluntarily reduced their consumption and to see whether this has had any effect on their wellbeing.

The active shunning of excessive consumption by some individuals and groups has a long history. Variously described as asceticism, voluntary simplicity or more recently as downshifting, this behaviour recognises that the adoption of a "more is better" philosophy of wealth and consumption doesn't provide the answer. From pre-biblical times, asceticism has been advocated by monks, Greek philosophers, economists, religious groups and financial planners. Spanning time, nationality and diverse religious beliefs, individuals have been singled out for their thoughts on the subject. John the Baptist, Epicurus, Henry David Thoreau and Mahatma Gandhi are just a few. As opposed to imposed poverty, the adoption of these values by these historical identities was voluntary.

One group, Bohemians, became conspicuous in Western Europe and the United States early in the nineteenth century. Their values were adopted by people spanning a broad spectrum of social classes — rich, poor, professional or unemployed. Values based on artistic and emotional appreciation were placed ahead of values based upon business success and conspicuous consumption. Bohemians held the bourgeoisie in contempt for their obsession with wealth accumulation. Bohemians felt that this pursuit provided little emotional fulfilment. Since living a Bohemian existence spanned financial classes, they denied the need to compete or impress on a financial basis. Fulfilment was sought through other avenues, such as time spent with others in mutual appreciation of art, nature, life and human intellectual and emotional interaction. Because these values didn't rely on appreciation of money, Bohemians freed themselves from materialistic pursuit.

In 1854 a book was first published entitled *Walden; or, Life in the Woods* by Henry David Thoreau, an American author, naturalist and philosopher. Thoreau's book described his thoughts, feelings and philosophies derived while living for more than two years in a simple cabin in woodland in Massachusetts, USA. Thoreau lived a very basic existence supplying himself only with the four necessities of life: food, shelter, clothing and fuel. He lived alone, spending much of his time reading and writing but didn't deny social interaction with visitors and friends. Thoreau felt that by separating himself from society he could better consider what constituted worthy values. He concluded that Americans were misdirected in their obsession for material success. He criticised man's tendency for conformity when he stated:

"If a man does not keep pace with his companions perhaps it is because he hears a different drummer. Let him step to the music he hears, however measured or far away."[20]

Despite the esteem and respect held for Thoreau's writings and ideals, it seems that the bulk of modern society forges forward largely unaware or uninfluenced by his thoughts. However, fortunately, not all.

Some groups accept voluntary simplicity and advocate its benefits. They consciously shun high levels of consumption even though it is available to them. Some individuals have chosen to reduce their working hours, change to a lower paying but more satisfying job, change careers or stop working altogether. Reasons for doing this include reducing stress, bringing balance into life, enabling more time to be spent with friends and family and respect for the environment by conspicuously reducing consumption. The term commonly used to describe this is downshifting and the people who do this are termed "downshifters". It represents a practical reversal of income amnesia and acknowledges that an increasing income, if totally consumed, provides little benefit.

Finally be conscious of the effect of income amnesia and remember that the most powerful tool to combat it is to "pay yourself first". Routinely divert an affordable proportion of your take home income to a separate bank account. Don't touch it for any reason other than to use the accumulated funds for investment. Unless genuinely required, divert any pay increases or additional windfall amounts into the same savings account before they are spent.

CHAPTER 10

The truth is in the numbers

"There are two ways of solving money problems.
Augment your means or diminish your wants."

BENJAMIN FRANKLIN

L et's add some powerful evidence to the concept that saving and investing are worthwhile pursuits. There is no better way to crystallise this thinking than to have numbers staring back at you from the page. There is power in quantifying the potential outcome of your actions rather than vaguely dreaming of what might be. To be able to plan a course from now to success and to map out what needs to be done each step of the way adds a degree of certainty that allows a confidence of pursuit that might otherwise be lacking. This chapter discusses how to establish the pool of investments that will provide a passive income stream.

The only certain way to financial independence is to save regularly and invest wisely. Let's emphasise the word "certain" because there are other but riskier routes. Also, and very importantly, almost anyone is capable of achieving this. The naysayers will quickly challenge this by saying that only high income earners are capable of saving. This just isn't true. This common misconception must be dispelled. It is hoped that the earlier chapters have provided some background to help reject this myth and this chapter will dispel it further. Certainly, someone with beer tastes and a champagne income will find that they can set aside larger amounts for saving and therefore achieve their target earlier, but even those with a relatively small income can get there too. Whatever your income it must never be forgotten that the key to success is to live within your means.

Now we come to calculating the amount of savings that will be required to supply you with an adequate flow of investment income. All other things being equal the level of income will be proportional to the size of the final pool. To receive an income of $100,000 per annum requires invested capital twice the size of that required to receive $50,000 per annum. Here then is the first step. You must quantify what you wish your ultimate level of passive income to be. For example, is it $50,000 per annum, $100,000 per annum or $300,000 per annum? Only you can determine this figure. Obviously the lower it is the easier it will be to achieve.

What then of inflation and the time value of money? While $100,000 per annum might be adequate for your current needs, it clearly won't be enough over time in an inflationary environment. In order to maintain purchasing parity your income will need to increase at least in line with inflation. To achieve this, the accumulated capital will need to be invested in asset classes that over time keep pace with general price increases. Two asset classes that have consistently demonstrated this characteristic over the long term have been real estate and stocks. Therefore either or both of these assets should be the predominant assets in any portfolio of investments. Property ownership need not necessarily be direct. Listed and unlisted property trusts (Real Estate Investment Trusts or "REITs") allow property investments to be made without the need to undertake lumpy direct acquisitions. However, a word of warning is required here. If an investment is made in a listed property trust check first the quality of properties in its portfolio and the level of borrowings utilised within its financing structure. Investors in listed property trusts saw their investments evaporate in 2008 as property prices collapsed worldwide. Property fund managers had used excessive levels of debt to fund property purchases. By way of example a 30 per cent drop in property prices will see an investment property portfolio that is funded with 70 per cent debt become worthless overnight.

Having chosen the desired level of passive income, the next step is to calculate the amount of capital required to provide this level of income. This is a relatively simple step. It is necessary to divide the required income by the yield that is provided by the chosen investment class. For example, if the net annual yield on the chosen property investment pool is seven per cent and the desired income flow is $100,000 per annum, then $100,000 ÷ 0.07 or $1,428,000 of debt free property needs to be held. Alternatively, if the grossed-up dividend yield on a portfolio of stocks is six per cent and the desired income is $70,000 then $70,000 ÷ 0.06 or $1,167,000 of stock needs to be held. You now have a target or a goal for your saving programme. The setting of a goal is essential since a destination is rarely reached unless it is defined. Note however that the target is in today's dollars. In an inflationary environment the target must be adjusted annually so as to allow for increases in the cost of living. In this regard monies already invested will look after themselves if invested in the appropriate asset classes. However, both the target itself and the ongoing regular contributions must be adjusted upwards to take inflation into consideration. Target resetting could appropriately be done on an annual basis in line with the inflationary environment experienced.

Given the target it is now possible to calculate how much needs to be saved each year in order to reach it. Clearly, the further into the future that the goal lies, the easier it will be to achieve — for two reasons. Firstly, less needs to be saved each week or month in order to achieve the total since there will be more saving periods. But secondly, and very importantly, the money already invested will provide an income flow from day one. This money is then reinvested. This reinvested income provides a powerful boost to savings. As time progresses the power of compounding ensures that this boost gains momentum until it actually has the potential to become the overwhelming force driving the savings forward. Long forgotten by most, despite it being taught at primary school, the power of compound interest is significant. Described by Albert Einstein as the greatest mathematical discovery of all time, it relies on the reinvestment of income flows generated from the growing pool of funds already invested.

Saving need not go on forever. When the target is reached income flows can then be used for consumption and as long as the principal is not touched an infinite flow of inflation adjusted income is established.

Let's return then to the method used to obtain the fuel which feeds this fire, the fuel being savings, more importantly the unrecognised savings potential of middle and lower income earners. Few people on these incomes realise they have the potential to accumulate a significant amount of money. Yet they have, given the combination of self-discipline and time. They fail to appreciate that wealth accumulation occurs over an extended time frame. However, if they have time then they have the power of compound interest working for them. They also fail to appreciate that small but regular increments do, over time, accumulate to very large sums. How then does someone who feels that he has no capacity to save find these small regular increments? Importantly he needs to analyse his current expenditure. Everybody can identify one form or another of regular discretionary spending which occurs in their lives. It could include anything from cigarettes, a pay TV subscription, gym membership, newspaper or magazine subscriptions, bought lunches or even a daily coffee. Don't discount the little things. If they occur regularly then they have the potential to amount to sizeable sums over extended periods. The low income earner who smokes a packet of cigarettes a day is denying his ability to become a millionaire. As is the person who buys a sandwich for lunch instead of bringing it from home, and who then washes it down with a caffé latte, while reading the daily newspaper.

Table 1 shows a list of 10 typical items that a hypothetical middle income earner has chosen to eliminate from discretionary spending. For many the magnitude of the dollar amounts in the columns is initially surprising. It needs to be stressed that many people are oblivious to how much they actually spend on recurrent discretionary items. These will be the very people who deny that the figures are possible. But remember two things in reading this table. Firstly that these are annualised figures. For example the figure for wine consumption represents only $35 per week which for many people is conservative. And secondly remember that this person's spending habits are not yours. Whilst you might not spend $50 per week on dining out (again a conservative figure for many) there is little doubt that you will have your own areas of non essential spending not represented by anything on this list. If you undertake some self-analysis then you might be surprised by the result.

Table 1 — Annual cost of discretionary spending

Item	Annual Cost $	Grossed Up Then Super Tax Rate Applied
Cigarettes	4,015.00	5,834.00
Chewing gum	547.50	795.00
Newspaper	547.50	795.00
Bought sandwich	1,501.50	2,182.00
Coffee	1,277.50	1,856.00
Gym membership	1,500.00	2,179.00
Pay TV	1,000.00	1,453.00
Reduction in dining out	2,600.00	3,778.00
Golf club	4,000.00	5,812.00
Reduction in wine consumed	1,825.00	2,652.00
Total		$27,336.00

(Superannuation tax rate = 15 per cent versus the chosen personal tax rate of 41.5 per cent)

These incremental amounts, if saved and invested, can accumulate to staggering amounts of money. Hard to believe? Then let's do the maths. The following calculations are based on the scales that were applicable at the time of writing but clearly might need to be altered to reflect changes in government tax policy and differing personal circumstances. They also assume that the hypothetical individual salary sacrifices the money into the more favourably taxed superannuation environment instead of choosing to save using after-tax dollars. Remember that until now this person has been unable to save hence was destined to work until the age of 65 and then retire on a modest government pension.

Therefore, $27,336 per annum has been freed up for investment into superannuation. This individual, who had thought that he had no money available for investing, now has $27,336 per annum for this purpose. In order to derive a future figure for an accumulated pool of capital, we need to make various assumptions. Let's then make the following five valid assumptions:

1   The contributions will continue to be made over the entire investment period.

2   The capital already invested will grow in line with inflation. In reality it has been shown that capital gains associated with real estate and stocks typically outstrip inflation when measured over extended periods.

3   All income is reinvested rather than spent. This is a legal requirement of superannuation anyway.

4   The investment return used in calculations is a real rate of return (that is, the actual rate of return less the rate of inflation).

5   The investment is made in a diversified stock portfolio.

Point 4 requires further explanation. For an investment return to be meaningful it needs to be adjusted for inflation. This then allows the comparison of dollar amounts through time. One thousand dollars compounded over time using an inflation adjusted (i.e. real) rate of return allows for the calculation of a figure that relates to today's values, not some inflated figure that isn't representative of current day purchasing power. Therefore the rate of return applicable to an investment within a particular period must be reduced by the inflationary impact over that period in order to bring the dollar value back to parity.

In the example currently under consideration a conservative rate of return has been used. Professor Jeremy Siegel, in his book *Stocks for the Long Run* showed that the average compound real rate of return on US stocks from 1802-1997 was 7 per cent[21]. In a more recent period, from 1982-1997, he calculated it to be 12.8 per cent. For the purpose of the following calculations the more conservative long range return is used. Because similar long term stock market returns have been observed between Australia and the US Siegel's figures have been adopted for this hypothetical example. The compounding rate of 7 per cent has been grossed up to 7.6 per cent to reflect the fact that in Australia dividends are taxed at the more favourable rate of 15 per cent when the stock is held within a superannuation fund (as opposed to the corporate rate of 30 per cent).

Table 2 — Age-related savings

Age	Accumulated Savings (Current Dollars)
55 years	$2.88 million
60 years	$4.31 million
65 years	$6.38 million

Table 2 therefore shows the sum (in present day dollars) that would be accumulated by the hypothetical investor at various stages in his life if he had started this process of redirection of discretionary spending (as outlined in Table 1) from the age of 25. It assumes no savings other than sacrifices to discretionary income as listed. Remember also that in Australia (under current legislation) any superannuation income derived after a beneficiary turns 60 years old is tax free, so a capital pool of $4.31 million will provide for a very comfortable existence.

At this stage it is worth reminding you that this $4 million was not derived from some windfall, lottery win or inheritance. Nor was it accumulated as the result of achieving a highly salaried position. It was accumulated as the result of dispensing with several non-essential items of expenditure and redirecting the newly found cash flow into a tax effective saving and investment vehicle over an extended time frame. This can be achieved by virtually any employed person who is prepared to apply a little planning and discipline to his financial situation. As Charlie Munger reminded us in chapter 5, "This is such a no brainer".

Let's apply the discussion to the low income earner. For him there is likely to be less fat to trim. He is less able to make the same number of cuts to discretionary spending since he is likely to be undertaking less discretionary spending in the first place. But let us assume, as an example, that he smokes a packet of cigarettes a day. Since he is a low income earner he will also be within a low tax bracket. At the time of writing the level of tax that this low income earner would most likely have been paying (in Australia) was 31.5 per cent. After application of superannuation contributions tax of 15 per cent the annual contribution to superannuation purely from applying this single accumulated saving would be $5,000 per year. As a consequence of the power of compounding over a 40-year period, this would accumulate to more than $1 million (again in today's dollars)!

The reformed smoker has not only undertaken a change in behaviour that will guarantee a comfortable retirement but he has provided himself with a better chance of actually reaching retirement age. Similar calculations can be applied to any mix of discretionary items that you choose to eliminate from your life.

It is important to remember that the elimination of one or a number of discretionary items must be converted into savings. Abandoning an $11 a day habit will not be converted into a million dollars if all that happens is that the $11 is spent on something else. A system of automatic drawing should be set up to divert this money to the appropriate savings vehicle before it ends up in your pocket. Remember the adage "pay yourself first".

Part III:
Investing Money

CHAPTER 11

The Efficient Market Hypothesis

"Something that everyone knows isn't worth knowing."

BERNARD BARUCH

The fundamental aim of investing is to receive back more than you initially allocate. In the previous chapter we based our accumulation plan on investing in stocks that returned a seven per cent return on investment. The big problem lies in assessing whether you will actually invest wisely enough to generate this level of return. Future returns, either taken on a portfolio basis or for individual companies can only ever be estimates. The reality is that in the case of stock market investment you just don't know for sure what the future cash flows are going to be. So if you don't know how much you are going to get back then how do you go about calculating the price which you should pay for the stock today?

Despite this difficulty you would expect that someone must be working out these prices, otherwise how could a price be struck at all? In fact many people do work out these prices. They are called investment analysts. But since they are dealing with the unknown, analysts can get it wrong as often as they get it right. Apart from them most people tend to just accept the market price as being the correct measure of value and don't really give it much more thought. They base their actions, their purchases, their sales on what the market is telling them at that point in time. But what if the market is wrong? What if it values assets correctly some of the time and incorrectly the rest of the time? Let's look at whether the market gets it right or gets it wrong.

In considering the accuracy of the market as a pricing mechanism a good starting point is to discuss the Efficient Market Hypothesis (EMH). It proposes that the price as quoted by the market reflects, at any point in time, all known information about that stock and therefore is the best estimate of the value of that stock. It implies that any attempt by an individual to calculate an independent valuation is futile. It has already been "calculated" and is reflected in the current market price.

It is based on the logic that mispricing of a stock would be quickly corrected by market participants. An underpriced stock would be bid up to fair value by opportunistic buyers. Similarly, overpriced stocks would be sold by sellers who recognised the overpricing. Since the market is made up of myriads of participants, some of whom have based their purchase or sale decisions on independent research, it is argued that the market price has come about as the result of an amalgamation of broadly considered rational thought. It goes on to add that an uninformed investor is protected within this environment since the price of any stock is in a constant state of adjustment to fair value as a result of the actions of the informed. Taking the argument further, it can be stated that an individual need not perform research on any stock in an effort to achieve superior returns since it is not possible to beat the market. Opportunities to benefit from market mispricing are just not available. There is a certain irony in this line of thinking. If everybody believed that the market was efficient and that attempts at research and valuation were futile, then no research would be undertaken. Based on the Efficient Market theorists' very own argument this would lead to market inefficiency. Therefore, in accepting the theory the true believers are relying on the fact that enough people don't believe it and so carry on with their independent research.

The term Efficient Market Hypothesis is attributed to Chicago professor Eugene Fama. Fama studied, researched and developed the concept subsequently writing papers in the 1960s and 1970s. Fama's PhD thesis, published in the January 1965 issue of the "Journal of Business", concluded that stock price movements were random and therefore unpredictable. Fama developed the concept of market pricing efficiency both theoretically and empirically and is often referred to as the father of the Efficient Market Hypothesis.

It is not Fama who derived the concept. Written records describing the concept predate Fama's work by 75 years. It was mentioned in print in 1889 by George Gibson who wrote:

(when) "shares become publicly known in an open market, the value which they acquire may be regarded as the judgement of the best intelligence concerning them."[22]

Also credited for his work in this area is French mathematician Louis Bachelier. He wrote a thesis in 1900 entitled "A Theory of Speculation" which argued that changes in option prices are fundamentally unpredictable.[23] It stated that "the mathematical expectation of the speculator is zero". By this he meant that the chance of an option increasing in price (in the short term) was the same as the chance of it decreasing. Whilst this thesis referred to price changes of options on government bonds its concepts have been extended to stock price movements. Of course in the long term the holder of stocks could expect an increase in prices as a result of the long term tendency for company earnings to increase. However, for the short term speculator the price movement is unpredictable. Bachelier, like Fama six decades later, was arguing that markets are efficient; that prices embody all that is known at that point in time. Since any future information is unknown, and could therefore impact on the price in either a positive or a negative manner, future price movements are unpredictable.

Bachelier died in 1946, his theory largely ignored by the financial world. However in 1954 an American statistician, Leonard Savage, came across Bachelier's thesis in a library and subsequent to reading it sent postcards to a number of people who he felt might be interested in reading it also. One of the postcards was sent to Paul Samuelson, an economist at the Massachusetts Institute of Technology (MIT). Samuelson, who was already interested in the concept of market efficiency was most interested in Bachelier's ideas. He became a strong advocate of the efficiency of markets in pricing of assets.

The Efficient Market Hypothesis was a ray of hope for many investors. Here was an apparently logical argument being put forward that freed them from any need to understand what they were doing. They could purchase stocks at random with the same chance of investment success as that which could be achieved by experienced market professionals. They were free from the need to undertake any research of their own and if they lost money they could blame the market.

This thinking was fine as long as the theory worked but the reality is that it has regularly failed to accurately explain observed market movements. By way of example on October 19, 1987 the US stock market shed approximately one quarter of its value in a single trading session. Similar shocks were seen worldwide. No universally and accepted reason has been identified for the collapse. How can it be argued, as it is under the Efficient Market Hypothesis, that prices have moved in response to new information, when no-one can identify what that information was! October 1987 is not an isolated event. There have been, over the last four centuries, many occasions when markets have moved sharply in response to minor or non-identifiable causes.

The Efficient Market Hypothesis also fails to explain why some investors consistently outperform the market. One group of investors that is put forward as evidence against the concept of market efficiency is that of the "value investors". This group doesn't accept that fair value and market value are always aligned. Undertaking their own process of valuation, they look for companies that are undervalued by the market and buy only when these opportunities are present. If the market was truly efficient then consistent outperformance by value investors could only be put down to luck.

If their success is being put down to luck then let's hear what some well known value investors have had to say in their own defence. John Maynard Keynes, Ben Graham and Warren Buffett have each used the technique of value investing to achieve superior returns. It is not surprising that each has discredited absolute market efficiency since in accepting the concept they would have been discrediting their own investment performance.

Keynes, apart from managing his own finances, was responsible for investment decisions relating to the King's College (Cambridge) Chest Fund. Between 1931 and 1945, by investing in stocks, Keynes achieved a near ten-fold increase in fund value. This return is even more impressive when it is noted that it was achieved without reinvestment of dividends. Over the same period the Standard & Poor's 500 Average remained flat and the London Industrial Average increased two-fold. Keynes had this to say of market efficiency:

> "It might have been supposed that competition between expert professionals, possessing judgement and knowledge beyond that of the average private investor, would correct the vagaries of the ignorant individual left to himself. It happens, however, that the energies and skill of the professional investor and speculator are mainly occupied otherwise. For most of these persons are, in fact, largely concerned, not with making superior long term forecasts of the probable yield of an investment over its whole life, but with foreseeing changes in the conventional basis of valuation a short time ahead of the general public."[24]

Or put another way, Keynes didn't believe that the majority of those supposed logical minds which were to be responsible for valuing the market in a disciplined, rational way were in fact doing so.

Ben Graham, the father of modern investing and author of the investment classics *Security Analysis* and *The Intelligent Investor*, was Warren Buffett's mentor and lecturer at Columbia University. Ben Graham, when lecturing on the discord between fair value and market value, used to speak of a hypothetical business partner called Mr Market. Mr Market would, each day, offer a price for your share of the jointly owned business. Some days his offer would be high, some days low. His offers were influenced by his bipolar mood swings. You could reject his offer on any day but the next day he would always be back with a new one. Graham's analogy served to stress to his students the discrepancy between market value and fair value and that the former was subject to significant mood affected change.

Graham knew that market prices were influenced by human sentiment but did acknowledge that market prices were not driven totally by irrational behaviour. He said this of market pricing:

> "… the market is not a weighing machine, on which the value of each issue is recorded by an exact and impersonal mechanism, in accordance with its specific qualities. Rather should we say that the market is a voting machine, whereon countless individuals register choices which are the product partly of reason and partly of emotion."[25]

Over time the market tends to be a weighing machine in that business success and improved returns are reflected in price. However, over shorter time frames the market price is "voted" to be higher or lower than "true weight".

The Efficient Market Hypothesis should not be totally discredited. It makes intuitive sense that the combined efforts at valuation by analysts and investors would tend to bring market value towards fair value. That market value is at times higher than fair value and at times lower should also be appreciated. The Efficient Market theorists were clearly onto a good concept. But there is a strong body of resistance to the concept that intrinsic value and market value are always aligned. Commentary by Warren Buffett on this topic bridges the gap between the believers and non-believers:

> "Observing correctly that the market was frequently efficient, [many academics and investment professionals] went on to conclude incorrectly that it was always efficient. The difference between these propositions is night and day."

Buffett was saying that the combined efforts of price analysts tend to keep the market within sight of true value most of the time and indeed at times they may well be aligned, but it is wrong to conclude that they are always aligned.

Indeed Buffett can afford to have contempt for the Efficient Market purists. His investment returns have been stellar. Commencing his investment career in earnest in 1956, he obtained an average annual compound return of just below 30 per cent from 1956 to 1969 and a 24 per cent average from 1969 to 2000. The US stock market average return over the same period was 12 per cent. If returns are capitalised over this 31-year period it shows that he outperformed the market by 160 times!

It has been argued by some that Buffett's success has been due to chance. Anyone who has studied elementary statistics understands the concepts of the bell curve and standard deviations from the mean. It has been claimed that Buffett's success represents a statistical outlier; that he is several deviations from the mean, an extremely rare but possible event.

At Columbia University in 1984 in what is considered a classic Buffett speech, he answered the sceptics. Buffett's speech formed part of the commemoration on the fiftieth anniversary of the book *Security Analysis*, written by Ben Graham and David Dodd. In delivering his speech, Buffett spoke of a national coin-flipping contest. If 225 million Americans each wagered a dollar in a one-on-one instant death contest whereby a successful flip on one day meant that you progressed to the next, Buffett put forward that in 20 days time there will be 215 contestants remaining, each with a little over $1 million in earnings. At the end of the contest the last remaining contestant would hold the total $225 million. He added that a business school professor would argue that the same result would have been achieved if 225 million orang-utans had engaged in a similar exercise, so insinuating that Buffett's results could be put down to chance.

But Buffett put forward an extremely powerful argument against chance being the reason for his success. If it had been due to chance alone then the existence of any other successful investors would be randomly distributed. That is, they would have nothing in common with Buffett himself other than the fact they were investors. However,

Buffett had a strong link with a number of other successful investors that put chance so far outside the realms of statistical possibility that as an explanation it could effectively be ignored. He explained the link as one of intellectual origin — a disproportionate number of investors were from a hypothetical village called Graham and Doddsville. They all followed and practised Ben Graham's principles of value investing. The fact that these disciples could so soundly outperform the market puts a large hole in the argument put forward by the proponents of the Efficient Market Hypothesis.

By way of concluding this topic of discussion it is amusing to consider the story of two hypothetical Efficient Market theorists who spot a $100 note on the footpath whilst walking down the street. Rather than picking it up they walk past it, reasoning that if it were real it would have been picked up already.

CHAPTER 12

Emotion and decision-making

"I can calculate the motions of the heavenly bodies but not the madness of people."

SIR ISAAC NEWTON

ewton made the above comment during the famed eighteenth century financial bubble associated with the South Sea Company. He was indicating that it was human emotion driving stock prices at that time not anything based on logic. In the 300 years since Newton made this observation, very little has changed. Indeed since 1602 when it was first possible to own and trade shares in a publically held company minds have been both fascinated with and incapable of fully understanding the gyrations of stock prices.

John Maynard Keynes, Ben Graham and Warren Buffett are all men both past and present who well understood how the market can misprice financial assets. Each recognised that true (intrinsic) value and the quoted market price were often misaligned. Each realised that this potential discrepancy could at times be extreme and that the principal forces driving this misalignment were our greatest weaknesses — emotional fragility and social conformity.

To be able to read emotions — both in ourselves and of those around us — is an important step in becoming a successful investor. Emotional fragility affects all aspects of our lives and it is important to understand how this can interfere with the process of rational thought. Consider the lovesick individual who boards a plane in pursuit of an absent partner. Pre-existing commitments such as going to work, university or attending to family life disappear as emotion overrules and the individual reacts in a manner that can be totally out of character.

Emotions can be responsible for extremes of behaviour. Envy and jealousy have been described as motives for murder. Pride can prevent the acceptance of an attractive offer. Anger can cause people to say things they don't mean. Euphoria can incite risk-taking behaviour. Depression can drive the young and talented to suicide.

Emotion has an all-pervasive effect on how we behave and how we react to our environment. Expressed in the common vernacular we sometimes "just aren't thinking straight".

Emotions can influence anyone's behaviour at any time, under a variety of circumstances. Let's apply this to the financial setting. For many people money is a very emotional topic. It has been known to induce people to marry, to divorce, to deceive and to kill. People link an excess or a lack of it to their own self-image. People crave it, people dream about it. Yet equally many people would deny that they fall prey to any of the above. Clearly money evokes some very complex emotional issues. It is not surprising that many investors fall prey to emotional influences.

Not only are there emotions which are directly associated with the investment process itself but there are a multitude of other pre-existing emotional conditions which have the potential to influence the individual's decision-making capacity. The individual might be tired, medicated, depressed, euphoric, going through a divorce or simply emotionally unstable to start with. These are a bad base from which to make investment decisions.

Secondly there are many emotional issues which come about as part of the investment experience itself. You need to appreciate what these are and they will be discussed in detail later on.

That emotions can interfere with our ability to make sound investment decisions has been recognised by one of investment's greats, Warren Buffett. In the preface to Benjamin Graham's book *The Intelligent Investor*, Buffett stated:

> "To invest successfully over a lifetime does not require a stratospheric IQ, unusual business insights, or inside information. What's needed is a sound intellectual framework for making decisions and the ability to keep emotions from corroding that framework."[26]

It could be argued that the emotions experienced by individuals should not have an impact on general stock prices. The market is made up of millions of participants each with their own individual psychological make-up. Some will be strong, some will be weak, some confident, some fearful. Looked upon as a whole, should not these characteristics even out? Or put another way, cannot a market be rational even though many of its participants at any particular time are acting irrationally? Are not enough people behaving rationally at any point in time so as to render the market rational?

The reality is that our emotional and psychological make-up leads us to act en masse. When we don't know an answer we look to the group to supply it. Mass emotion can and does move markets.

Often the market misprices financial assets and at times significantly so. Faced with that mispricing we are often unable to respond appropriately. We look to everyone else for guidance and just do as they do.

As previously stated most people have very little and often no idea of the true value of the asset which they are purchasing or selling. In response to the concept of market mispricing some would reply that "The true value of something is what others will pay for it; hence is not the market price its true value?" Yes it is but only if you need to transact an order for that stock on that day.

As mentioned stock valuation is an imprecise process. Unlike the valuation of bonds, future cash flows are uncertain (indeed how long the company will remain in business is uncertain). Even the great investors Ben Graham and Warren Buffett have commented on the difficulty that they have experienced in the valuation process. They have both allowed for this pricing uncertainty by utilising a concept they have referred to as "a margin of safety". This states that since it is impossible to derive an accurate present value utilising the discounted values of as yet unknown future cash flows, they compensate for this by setting their buy price at a discount to the value which they have calculated as fair. Therefore allowance is made for uncertainty. A "margin of safety" is introduced. So if those with exceptional skills, those who have devoted their lives to the valuation process, those who have "put the score on the scoreboard of financial success" can get no closer than an educated "guesstimate" then what hope has the rest of the general investment population?

CHAPTER 13

Intelligence doesn't guarantee success

"If you don't know who you really are, the stock market is an expensive place to find out."

ADAM SMITH

A point that needs to be stressed is that possession of a high intellect is no guarantee of success when it comes to investing. Whilst a sharp mind helps in developing a sound framework of investment principles, investment success is by no means guaranteed by or restricted to those with a superior IQ. Indeed many highly intelligent people have failed at the investment game due to either a lack of certain personal qualities or a failure to apply important investment principles.

It has already been stated that there are four main areas where an individual needs to have skill in the management of money. These are namely the making, saving, investing and enjoyment of that money. It can be stated further that failure in any one area usually results in failure overall. Most people are preoccupied with the first, that is making it. Indeed, many people are very good at making it but commonly fail at one and sometimes all three of the other facets. Many of these people come to public prominence because of a particular skill commonly related to sport, commerce or show-business. Alternatively they may have come to public prominence solely because of their high income or high consumption habits. Many are quite intelligent but many don't get past first base in terms of financial success. They can make money but fail to save, invest or enjoy it. This chapter will concentrate on investment failure, having previously discussed factors associated with the failure to save.

As he is the most successful investor who has ever lived, Warren Buffett's comments in relation to this topic bear repeating:

> "To invest successfully over a lifetime does not require a stratospheric IQ, unusual business insights, or inside information. What's needed is a sound intellectual framework for making decisions and the ability to keep emotions from corroding that framework."

As part of establishing the sound intellectual framework that Warren Buffett is referring to it is necessary to put in some effort to learn how and why financial markets move. And having gained that knowledge it is necessary to hold a firm belief in those principles. Use them as the basis for making investment decisions rather than simply taking your cue from what everyone else might be doing at that time.

There are many high profile and intelligent people who have been found lacking in financial intelligence. By way of example it is worth noting a few well documented examples. Sir Isaac Newton (1643-1727) no doubt possessed an exceptional intellect. The famed Englishman was a physicist, mathematician, astronomer, alchemist and philosopher. He enunciated the principles of momentum, invented the reflecting telescope, discovered how white light broke into the spectrum, theorised on the development of the stars and developed calculus and the binomial theorem. French mathematician, Joseph Louis Legrance described him as "the greatest genius who ever lived". It is therefore interesting to note Newton's folly in the financial markets of his time.

Near the end of Newton's life England was caught in the grip of a speculative financial mania known as the South Sea Bubble. The South Sea Company, having been created by Robert Harley, Earl of Oxford, in 1711, was granted limited trading rights with South America. Unrealistic profit projections fuelled speculation which developed into a national fascination in stock trading. This encouraged the establishment of many new companies both real and fictitious and a contagion of financial fraud. It all came crashing down in September 1720 when financial reality bit. The supremely intelligent and rational Sir Isaac noted in the spring of 1720, before the market crashed:

"I can calculate the movement of the heavenly bodies but not the madness of people."

Accordingly, on April 20, 1720, and before the market crashed, he sold his shares in the South Sea Company for a £7,000 profit. However, as rational a mind as can be accredited to him, he made the mistake of re-entering the market. It would appear that he was influenced by the mass speculative hysteria that had infected the nation. He had succumbed to the "madness of people" that he had earlier described. The market crashed to earth in September 1720 and Sir Isaac lost £20,000.

Irving Fisher (1867-1947) was an American economist, considered perhaps to be the first celebrity economist. He was Professor of Economics at Yale University, the founder of Modern Capital Theory and a multimillionaire. His financial analyses and forecasting were eagerly sought. On October 15, 1929, just 13 days prior to Black Monday, Fisher was quoted as saying:

"Stock prices have reached what looks like a permanently high plateau."

Over the 32 months following this statement the US stock market declined by nearly 90 per cent from its 1929 peak. The Dow Jones Index didn't reach its 1929 peak again until 1954, 25 years later. Clearly Fisher's prophecy proved to be grossly inaccurate. Yet here was an intelligent man with a deep seated education in economics and financial markets who had made a significant misjudgment. What was his error? It was perhaps in falling prey to the general mood at that time. Fisher was working on a book in which he argued that advances in scientific processes and business production resultant from new invention and research meant that significant growth in corporate earnings could be expected. The cautious investor would have been concerned in 1929 that price earnings (P/E) ratios were particularly high when compared with historical averages. However, using Fisher's argument the high P/Es could be justified because he said that future growth in earnings would compensate for the high purchase prices of listed stocks. It is not the only time that there has been strong belief in new technologies as the provider of accelerated levels of earnings and on each occasion subsequent events have shown that the optimism was unfounded.

Bob Shiller identified four periods in the 120 year period between 1881 and 2000 when P/E ratios were way above their long term average of 15.[27] These were in 1901, 1929, 1966 and 2000. On each occasion there was extreme optimism regarding the potential growth in earnings that new technologies could deliver. Improved machines, transport and information flows result in improved efficiencies and greater corporate profitability. Whilst neither improvements in technology nor economic growth are linear, they are certainly closer to being linear than the manic booms and busts seen periodically in stock market price movement. It would appear that in 1929 Fisher had fallen hostage to the trap of justifying the high prices by looking for an argument that supported this situation rather than recognising that prices were just simply too high. The financial graveyard is littered with the bodies of investors who justified market prices with arguments that ultimately proved to carry no weight.

Richard Band, in his book *Contrary Investing for the '90s*, wrote:

> "A symptom of a dying boom is a widespread rejection of old standards of value. According to the apologists for the boom, the dawning of a new era makes today's high prices reasonable, even cheap, no matter how outrageous they would have seemed only yesterday."[28]

Irving Fisher felt that a new era justified the high prices seen in 1929. Using Warren Buffett's criterion for successful investment, it would seem that Fisher, as knowledgeable about investment markets as he was, was unable to stop emotions from corroding his intellectual framework. He accepted the inflated prices as normal. This is an extremely common human reaction. Rapid price increases can occur in relation to any commodity. For example, real estate prices might double in the space of a few years. If a potential purchaser was advised at the start of the period that they would soon need to pay double the current price for a house then they would likely express disbelief. But given the price shift and a general increase in the market value of all real estate, then the same person might consider the price at the beginning of the period to have been remarkably cheap and the current (higher) price reasonable. People rapidly adjust their perception of value to align with current prices no matter how much they have changed. The same tends to hold true for stock prices.

In January 2000 the bull market driven by the optimism associated with internet stocks was reaching its peak. The average price earnings ratio associated with stocks in the S&P Composite Stock Price Index was in excess of 40 times. This was way above the long term average of 15 times and exceeded the highs of 1901, 1929 and 1966. There was widespread confidence that technology would deliver growth in corporate earnings. Whilst earnings growth did ultimately provide a degree of justification for the higher than average P/Es for many established companies, what was most disturbing was what was happening with internet stocks. Many of these start-up companies had never produced a profit yet were trading at breathtaking prices. The reason: excessive market exuberance. A mania had developed. Market prices far exceeded values derived by conventional methods of valuation. In many cases conventional methods of valuation could simply not be applied due to a lack of profits as analytical input. Analysts needed to find a new valuation technique that would justify the prevailing high market prices.

The traditional method whereby earnings were capitalised by applying a P/E multiple to after tax earnings had to be adapted. In order to value the internet companies, many of which were losing money, it was proposed that they be valued by multiples of revenue.

Therefore loss making companies could be valued on the basis of how much product they were selling. The costs of doing business were excluded from the calculation. Often this led to the ridiculous situation whereby the more money they lost the higher was their market value. In reflecting on this bizarre state of affairs US satirist and author P.J. O'Rourke stated:

> "E-commerce eliminates the nuisance of having to make a profit. This has been the stumbling block to businessmen for years. Now, however, Amazon.com can lose money on everything it sells and make their money selling it back to Wall Street."

In line with Irving Fisher's thinking and Richard Band's warning, the Australian business newspaper *The Financial Review* carried an article on January 4, 2000 only weeks before the internet bubble burst. It stated that:

> "The rapid technological changes that are transforming the economic underpinnings of the United States are leading to rarely seen dynamics … The phenomenon in the US has been dubbed the 'new paradigm'."

In 2000 not only were investors accepting the inflated prices but so-called experts and market commentators had adjusted their thinking and were putting forward their own arguments to justify them. In borrowing Buffett's words, their framework had been corroded. Less than two years following *The Financial Review* article the NASDAQ index, which represented the bulk of the US internet and technology based companies, had fallen by over 70 per cent.

At the start of this chapter it was stated that the possession of high intelligence is no guarantee of success in the investment process. By way of example Sir Isaac Newton, a person of supreme intelligence, was shown to have fallen prey to the effects of human emotion undermining the process of successful investment decision-making. Sir Isaac Newton was a scientist, not a financial analyst, but Irving Fisher, who was both intelligent and a follower of the financial markets, was also swept up in the euphoria of the "here and now" of the capital markets in 1929.

In 1993 John Meriwether, a former head of bond trading at the US based investment bank, Solomon Brothers, formed a hedge fund called Long Term Capital Management (LTCM). It began trading in February 1994 with start-up capital of over $1 billion. To say that the investment team was experienced would have been a gross understatement. Meriwether had attracted to the fold a team comprising some of Wall Street's elite traders. Its board included two Nobel Prize winning economists, namely Myron Scholes and Robert Merton. They shared the 1997 Nobel Memorial Prize in Economics for "a new method to determine the value of derivatives". Scholes was already well known within financial circles since the Black-Scholes equation for pricing options had gained wide acceptance and usage since he developed it in the 1970s with Fisher Black. Robert Merton had further expanded the Black-Scholes work.

The LTCM team had developed mathematical models with the aim of benefiting from changes in spreads between bond markets. Termed convergence trades, when yield spreads were high they bought high yield long dated bonds and sold lower yield long dated bonds. They aimed to close out their positions as yields narrowed. These strategies proved to be enormously successful, generating large profits for hedge fund members. For the first few years their fund was the talk of Wall Street and there was a general belief that LTCM was an invincible financial juggernaut. However, as LTCM's capital base grew larger, its traders started to undertake financial positions utilising strategies that were outside their area of expertise. In addition, they took out highly leveraged positions which introduced significant degrees of risk. By 1998 debt exceeded underlying capital by 26 times. Its off balance sheet derivative positions amplified this risk even more. In 1998 things turned particularly sour for LTCM. Turbulence in financial markets led to a divergence of bond yields in relation to the very positions that they had expected to converge. The fact that their positions were structured on the back of high leverage meant that their losses were amplified. LTCM lost heavily and fell into financial distress. Ultimately the Federal Reserve Bank of New York organised a financial bail-out for LTCM with major creditors putting up $3.625 billion. It was considered necessary in order to avoid a wider financial market collapse.

If as you read this book you feel discouraged with respect to your capability to forge a successful path through the investment world when even some of the market's elite have failed, be reassured. The traders who made up LTCM were no doubt brilliant mathematicians but investors they were not. They were speculators. The risks they were taking were further amplified as their speculation was being funded by highly leveraged positions, something that should be avoided by the "intelligent investor".

It is important that the difference between investment and speculation be understood. A speculator purchases or sells a financial asset with the aim of reversing that position for profit at a time, usually in the not too distant future. An investor purchases a financial asset for an indefinite period with a fundamental interest in its future cash flows, not just as a result of capital gain but also as a result of income flow. A speculator is less interested in value and is more interested in market price. An investor looks for value. In relating the difference between the two, Buffett had this to say:

> "What is 'investing' if it is not the act of seeking value at least sufficient to justify the amount paid? Consciously paying more for a stock than its calculated value — in the hope that it can soon be sold for a still higher price — should be labelled speculation…"

Ben Graham, in his classic text book *The Intelligent Investor*, had this to say of the difference between investment and speculation:

> "An investment operation is one which, upon thorough analysis promises safety of principal and an adequate return. Operations not meeting these requirements are speculative."

So in order to optimise the chance of success, the difference between what constitutes investment and what constitutes speculation must be understood. An activity commonly undertaken by the masses is the purchase of listed stocks in the hope that they will rise in price so that they can be sold for a capital gain. This is what drove Sir Isaac Newton to repurchase South Sea shares in 1720. It was Oscar Wilde who said that a speculator knows the price of everything and the value of nothing.

When Warren Buffett spoke of an investor requiring a sound intellectual framework, this framework was to include a perception of what constitutes value. Commonsense more so than high IQ is the personal quality that will keep an investor's feet on the ground when assessing value. The body of current opinion should not sway his thinking whilst assessing it.

CHAPTER 14

From tulips to the internet

"I know of no way of judging the future but by the past."

PATRICK HENRY (1775)

It appears that there is something innate in the human psyche that leads us to believe that we are the first to experience anything. Even if a similarity between current circumstances and the past is recognised there is a certain arrogance in the common qualification that this time the outcome will be different, or that society's current level of sophistication will mean that the situation will be handled in a more appropriate manner. The true student of history will recognise that, technological advances aside, there is little that is experienced in the present which has not already been experienced by those before us. And additionally, our reaction to those circumstances is rarely different to theirs. That many fail to recognise this fact is embodied in the following statement from American scholar and educator, Thomas R. Lownsberry who said that:

> "We must review with profound respect the infinite capacity of the human mind to resist the inroads of useful knowledge."

That our response to any situation is little different to the response shown by our predecessors, and that we fail to learn from their experiences is true in most areas of human endeavour and no less so in the arena of the financial markets. The reality is that the lessons of history provide the potential for a rich education, particularly in relation to the follies of human behaviour.

It is important to acknowledge that any market whether financial or other is influenced by human behaviour and it is equally important to realise that in this respect the forces that drove financial markets four centuries ago are similar to those which drive them today.

Since 1602 when the first trade in publically owned stock commenced in Amsterdam the same follies in human behaviour have been repeated again and again. To not recognise this is to ignore an important part of your financial education. There are some exceptional books on this subject hence no attempt should be made to emulate them but it is worth pursuing a brief discussion outlining the main financial follies that have occurred over the last 400 years.

TULIPOMANIA (1634-1637)

Tulipomania refers to a speculative bubble associated with the trade of tulip bulbs which occurred in Holland from 1634 to 1637. The primary source of information is a 1637 pamphlet published during the peak of the speculation. Other sources of information include numerous pamphlets which were published subsequent to 1637. The book most commonly associated with this topic is Charles Mackay's *Extraordinary Popular Delusions and the Madness of Crowds*. First published in 1841, it is still in print today.

The tulip was introduced into Western Europe from Turkey in the mid-sixteenth century. Initially purchased by the wealthy, it became a symbol of status. Typical of any symbol of status, the middle and working classes became interested in owning tulips as well. Price increases fuelled speculation until bulbs were more often bought for the purpose of obtaining a profit on resale than they were for cultivation. Interest ultimately became so intense that by 1634 people were leaving their normal employment in order to speculate solely on the price of tulip bulbs. Some people sold their homes in order to finance their purchase. Even a futures market in tulip bulbs developed whereby trade could occur without the need for physical delivery. As with all manias, issues related to value were largely ignored. Purchases were made in the sole hope of passing bulbs onto other speculators. In essence it was a game of pass-the-parcel whereby success relied on the ability to find someone to purchase your bulbs at a price higher than was paid and before the music stopped playing. The record sale price for a single bulb was attributed to a species called *Semper Augustus*, for which a price of 5,500 florins was paid. This was a time when the average annual salary of a Dutch worker was 150 florins. This was speculation pure and simple. When purchases are being made with no consideration for value, when the only motive is to on sell the items for capital gain, then the process cannot be described as investment. And this is as true with stocks, bonds or real estate as it is with tulip bulbs. For the tulip speculators value was irrelevant. Extreme price levels were reached as each successive purchase was made in the expectation that it could be on sold at a higher price. And prices kept rising as long as there were people who were willing to play the game. What drove these prices was human behaviour, human expectation, human weakness, human envy and human greed. We are no more immune to this behaviour now.

In the 1990s a new communications technology based on the internet was being adopted worldwide in an exponential manner. Technology stocks based on the use of the internet and expanded telecommunications networks were being priced at unrealistic and unsustainable levels. Again, as in the time of Tulipomania, value was ignored. Money was being made by speculators in internet stocks purely from buying and quickly on selling. As in the time of Tulipomania, people were leaving their normal jobs in order to become full time speculators in so-called "tech stocks". Television news showed images of ex-clerks, cleaners, teachers and engineers who had left their jobs and instead were spending their days at home in front of computer screens. They were buying and on selling stocks within time frames of hours or minutes. Termed day traders, they were relying on the same phenomenon that occurred during the period of Tulipomania — that there would always be someone ahead of you prepared to pay more than the price you paid. But when the music stops someone is always left standing. And in financial markets if all that is supporting a price is hope then when it ceases to be the prevailing emotion prices come crashing down.

THE MISSISSIPPI SCHEME (1719-1720)

The Mississippi Scheme occurred in France but its instigator was a Scotsman named John Law. Born the son of a wealthy goldsmith, he gained a significant inheritance at the age of 17 upon his father's death. Law, however, was more interested in gambling, travel and adventure than he was in settling down in Edinburgh hence he set off to London. Despite some early success with the cards he ultimately squandered his inheritance in London's gaming houses. In 1694 Law killed a man called Edward Wilson in a duel. He was brought to trial and sentenced to death. His life was later spared when the penalty was reduced but the family of the deceased chose to appeal the lighter decision. Law felt it was time to flee to the continent and with assistance he escaped from prison. He crossed the channel to Europe where he supported himself by gambling at which he ultimately developed significant skill. He possessed strong views in relation to economics and management of government finances, views which he expressed on a number of occasions to a regular gambling acquaintance, a Frenchman, the Duke of Orleans.

In 1715 the French King Louis XIV died and since the heir to the throne was only seven years old, the Duke of Orleans was appointed to manage the country's affairs. One particularly important task was to restore France's disastrous financial state. Poor financial management by Louis XIV had rendered France on the verge of financial collapse. Whilst financial solutions were being considered and tried, Law presented himself to his friend the Duke of Orleans, now the Regent. Incapable of managing financial affairs himself, the Regent received Law with enthusiasm. Law proposed the establishment of a bank and the issue of a paper currency. On May 5, 1716 Law was authorised, by way of a royal edict, to establish the bank under the name of Law and Company. Law's policies lifted the country's economic wellbeing.

The Regent granted Law control of a company which was awarded the exclusive rights of trade with the province of Louisiana along the River Mississippi. Imbued with confidence in Law as a financial manager and optimism as to the wealth to be obtained from commerce, a frenzy of speculation developed in the shares of the new Mississippi Company. In early 1719 the Mississippi Company was granted trading rights with the East Indies, China and the South Seas. Further stock was issued to the public. Over-subscribed by 6 to 1, Law's private home was under siege by eager stock applicants. The level of interest in stock was so great and so large were the crowds that clamoured to buy it Law was prompted to buy the Hôtel de Soissons which had a garden of several acres to provide a site for trading. The seller, Prince de Carignon, reserved the right to source profit from the leasing of tents and pavilions in the hotel gardens, the only sites from which stock trading was now allowed. It was estimated that the Prince subsequently generated monthly revenue in excess of 250,000 livres (£12,500) from the leasing of this space for stock speculation.

Market prices for Law's Mississippi stock rose dramatically from 500 livres in 1719 to as much as 15,000 livres in the first half of 1720, all despite the fact that the company was barely generating a profit. Value was ignored, a speculative bubble was in full swing. But all bubbles eventually burst and in the summer of 1720 there was a general decline in confidence. By 1721 the market capitalisation of the company had declined by 97 per cent from its highs. Prior to the company's demise Law had converted much of his paper wealth into real estate but he was forced to abandon his estates and flee when opinion turned against him. He died a poor man in Venice in 1729. Many of the speculators who had bought stock with no regard to value but with the sole aim of on selling for capital gain were financially ruined.

THE SOUTH SEA BUBBLE (1720)

While France was experiencing the speculative mania associated with Law and the Mississippi Scheme, England was experiencing its own bubble. It was centred round the South Sea Company, a company created by Robert Harley, Earl of Oxford in 1711. In a manner similar to the proposed activities of the Mississippi Company, it was granted rights to trade with South America. Unrealistic profit projections fuelled speculation and there developed a national fascination in stock trading.

When money is being easily made by some then others quickly try to emulate their success. The rise in the price of South Sea stock coupled with the near insatiable appetite for company stock of any kind saw many dubious schemes being proposed requesting the subscription of capital. Many of these proposals were bogus claims created solely for the purpose of extracting money from a gullible public. In a manner similar to the internet bubble of 2000, companies were raising capital that had little or no chance of success. Charles Mackay's book lists many of the schemes proposed during the time of the South Sea Bubble with a handful of the more ludicrous and amusing being listed below:

- A wheel of perpetual motion. Capital one million.
- For paying pensions to widows and others. Capital two millions.
- For erecting houses or hospitals for taking in and maintaining illegitimate children. Capital two millions.
- For buying and fitting out ships to suppress pirates.
- For extracting silver from lead.
- For the transmutation of quicksilver into a malleable fine metal.
- Puckles machine — for discharging round and square cannon balls and bullets, and making a total revolution in the art of war.

Added together, the total of all monies proposed for the bubble projects exceeded £300 million which was more than the value of all the land in England at that time.

In the markets of 1720, we can observe two classic forms of speculative behaviour that are still alive and well in today's financial markets. Firstly there is the game of "pass the parcel". An object need not possess any intrinsic value at all but be purchased if it is perceived that another person is likely to buy it from you at a higher price. This is what had happened during Tulipomania and it was happening again in the South Sea Bubble. Indeed some of the more financially astute of the time recognised that stocks of little or no value were being traded at inflated prices. A comment ascribed to Adam Anderson, a former cashier of the South Sea Company, was based on his belief that many purchasers of South Sea Company shares did so with the aim to:

> "rid of them in the crowded alley to others more credulous than themselves."

One of the more famous quotes associated with this time is that of an anonymous pamphleteer who expressed the following:

> "The additional rise of this stock above the true capital will be only imaginary; one added to one, by any rules of vulgar arithmetic, will never make three and a half; consequently, all the fictitious value must be at a loss to some persons or other, first or last. The only way to prevent it to oneself must be to sell out betimes, and so let the Devil take the hindmost."[29]

Here three centuries ago was someone telling us that as with the game of musical chairs, people will find themselves without a seat when the music stops. That the same happened as recently as March 2000, when the internet bubble burst, reinforces the fact that these are errors made by weaknesses in human thinking and will persist as long as humans and financial markets co-exist.

The second feature of the behaviour seen during the South Sea Bubble, which is no different from behaviour seen today, is the promotion of capital raisings for enterprises of dubious quality. Perhaps one of the most famous of bubble companies was one which was quoted in its prospectus to be:

> "A company for carrying on an undertaking of great advantage but nobody to know what it is."

The prospectus forecast earnings for each £100 share to be £100 per annum. Subscribers were requested to initially submit a deposit of £2 for each share. The promoter of this bogus company collected £2,000 in deposits within a period of one day and was never to be seen again.

No doubt the modern day reader would be amused to think that people would have been so gullible as to subscribe their money to what appeared to be such a fraudulent undertaking. But the reality is that greed, ignorance and gullibility are all unchanging features of human character. That the period under consideration is represented by a different century is of little consequence. People of the twenty-first century possess the same emotional and behavioural make-up that people did 300 years ago. Financial sophistication is overstated as an antidote to errors in financial judgment. Few of today's speculators actually possess a high level of financial sophistication but neither did all of yesterday's speculators lack it. What is really required at times of market exuberance is to have both feet firmly planted on the ground.

By way of an interesting comparison, if you believe that no-one today would be so gullible as to subscribe to a company on the basis of a prospectus that stated it was:

"A company for carrying on an undertaking of great advantage but nobody to know what it is."

then consider the words of a 1999 prospectus issued for a capital raising in association with a company called NetJ.Com at the height of the dot.com bubble. It stated that:

"The company is not currently engaged in any substantial activity and has no plans to engage in such activities in the foreseeable future."

The $110 million capital raising associated with the 1999 prospectus was oversubscribed. The stock price rose 18 fold within months of the offering after which it quickly came crashing down to earth. There was a total loss of investor capital. If only the subscribers to NetJ.Com had read Charles Mackay's book then they would have immediately identified a similarity between statements in the two prospectuses despite them having been penned 279 years apart.

CHAPTER 15

Creation of a bubble

"Don't believe everything you think."

(UNASCRIBED)

What causes a financial bubble? Is there an initiating factor, a spark? Does there need to be a particular sentiment prevailing to fuel a bubble's development?

One possible cause was proposed by US economist Hyman Minsky. Minsky was interested in what led to booms and busts both within an economy and financial markets. Minsky proposed that an event of "displacement" was the initiator of a speculative boom. The form that this displacement took could vary from one boom to another. Examples of a displacement could include:

- The invention or development of a new technology
- A significant shift in economic policy
- Greater affordability of credit as the result of a fall in interest rates
- Any change in a particular sector of the economy which resulted in people perceiving that sector more favourably.

The development of the internet is a case in point where the hope of improved corporate efficiencies and the development of new sales and distribution possibilities were perceived. In the case of the Mississippi Scheme and the South Sea Bubble, it was the promise of new trade opportunities between Europe and America which sparked interest. The inflated stock markets of 1901, 1929 and 1966 were initiated by advances in new technologies and the general expectation that this would significantly increase corporate profits. Stock prices of railway companies rose and crashed in the UK in the 1840s when railways captured the public imagination.

A shortage of nickel during the 1960s and a price peak in November 1969 saw a spectacular run up in the price of the Australian mining exploration company Poseidon. It caught the public's attention following an exploration find with the result that its stock price rose from 80¢ in September 1969 to in excess of $250 within the space of five months. The value of the exploration find was not in keeping with the market price so its stock price rapidly retreated by three quarters of its market high.

A displacement therefore provides hope to people of a new opportunity for making money. If enough people share this hope it becomes, at least initially, self-fulfilling as the price of the asset is bid up. Increased demand puts further pressure on prices and they continue to rise. As price increases gain momentum more people take notice and are drawn into the market. Stock market booms are also characterised by an increase in the number of initial public offerings. Even with this new supply of stock the growth in demand outstrips it. A simple economic principle is that a greater volume of money chasing a relatively fixed volume of assets will result in a rise in asset prices.

The new money doesn't come simply from investors dipping into savings. Capital limitations lead people to borrow in order to invest further. A common bull market phenomenon is the use of credit secured against stock held by the borrower (referred to as margin lending). In fact contrarian investors use a run up in margin lending as an indication of an impending market peak. It is interesting to observe the increased use of margin lending as an investment funding vehicle at times of market exuberance. In the run up to the crash of 1929 bank lending (on margin) rose from $1 billion in 1921 to $8.5 billion in 1929. Similar experiences have been seen in the Australian market. By way of a recent example Reserve Bank of Australia statistics show that in the eight years from September 1999 to

September 2007 margin lending increased by nearly 600 per cent from $5.2 billion to $35.9 billion. This corresponds with the general market indices more than doubling over the same period. Within a few weeks of the market's peak in November 2007 the market fell by in excess of 20 per cent; a year later it had fallen by 50 per cent. Margin calls followed the market downturn and leveraged investors started falling like flies.

Positive sentiment is reinforced at times of market exuberance as profitable trades are made. There is an old saying that a rising tide raises all boats. As the general market rises so too does the stock price of each of the companies within that market. Speculators become less discriminating in their purchases. The stock prices of the vast majority of listed companies appreciate in value independent of whether a rational valuation process would justify the rise. A tendency for overtrading develops whereby speculators switch from one stock to another. Because the market is moving up en masse, each stock is sold for a profit before a move is made to the next stock. Speculators fail to realise that it is not skill in stock picking rather a general rise in nearly all company stock prices which is providing the reward. Like the frog that jumps from one lily pad to the next, they aren't improving their position by action.

During the bull market phase there is an increasing level of interest in the stock market from people who otherwise wouldn't consider investing. What is it that provides those who understand little of the operation of financial markets with the confidence to enter the market in the first place? Few would have read Eugene Fama's dissertation on Market Efficiency hence, despite their inability to value companies, comfort could not have been obtained by a belief in the Efficient Market Hypothesis. Even more staggering is what provides the confidence for them to go one step further and borrow money not yet earned to wager on the chance that prices will continue to rise?

As part explanation, consider the following. You are walking down a long street. You appear to be the only person around until in the distance you see a person who is standing by the side of the kerb surrounded by paraphernalia. As you approach, you note that it is a man behind a street-side stall. Only you and he are present. He is selling watches pinned on makeshift boards. As you approach within talking range, he starts his sales pitch in the hope that you might stop and buy a wristwatch. You smile as politely as you dare so he doesn't misinterpret your manner as a display of interest, step up your pace, and keep walking past. You doubt the quality of his merchandise and don't feel any desire to make a purchase.

Consider now a different situation. You are walking along a crowded city street. People are sitting at street-side cafes, entering and leaving shops and there is a general bustle and noise associated with the environment. Just ahead a large crowd has gathered. Members of the crowd are pushing to the middle of the throng waving $20 notes in the air. People are leaving the scene with a general look of satisfaction on their faces. Upon entering the crowd you see that the interest is in a street-side stall where a man is selling watches. He has a polished banter advocating the value that can be bought for $20 apiece. As quickly as he lifts each watch in the air with one hand another $20 is pushed into the palm of his other hand. You get caught up in the enthusiasm of the moment. Twenty dollars seems a small price to pay for what many others perceive to be such good value. You gain confidence in the potential benefit of a purchase from the actions of those around you. So many others are providing confirmation that the decision is a good one that you too thrust $20 into the vendor's hand and leave the scene with a watch.

We gain confirmation from the behaviour of people around us. If people are making money in the stock market why can't we? This attitude is reinforced when we perceive that person to be our peer. It may be that it is a friend or a relative who we see experiencing success in their trading and we know that they are far from a market professional. If they can do it why can't we? But to gain confidence from the actions of people who are as equally ignorant as ourselves is far from rational behaviour and, given time, they will come unstuck.

Gustave Le Bon (1841-1931) was a French social psychologist and sociologist. His book *La Psychologie des Foules*, published in 1895 was translated into English the following year and released under the title *The Crowd, A Study of the Popular Mind*. It is still in print and is widely read by students of financial markets. The thrust of Le Bon's book is that an otherwise rational individual can behave in a totally irrational manner when part of a crowd.

To quote Le Bon:

> "The impulses which the crowd obeys are so imperious as to annihilate the feelings of personal interest — Pre-meditation is absent from crowds ..."

> "... the special characteristics of crowds are several — such as the impulsiveness ... incapacity to reason, the absence of judgement and of the critical spirit ..."

Le Bon is saying that within a crowd people stop thinking for themselves and take on the general view.

Le Bon's concept of a crowd is not one that necessitates everyone being in one place. He spoke of a "psychological crowd". This description is particularly relevant in financial markets since participants are not in a common place. The dissemination of information is today so rapid and widespread that the world can be thought of as a marketplace and the crowd as its worldwide participants. Le Bon spoke of this mental unity:

> "The disappearance of conscious personality and the turning of feelings and thoughts in a different direction ... do not always involve the simultaneous presence of a number of individuals on one spot. Thousands of isolated individuals may acquire ... the characteristics of a psychological crowd."

Le Bon's writings may also provide some insight as to why value is ignored at times of market exuberance. Why were traditional valuation principles ignored at the time of the dot.com bubble? Why did previously rational market analysts attempt to place values on seemingly worthless companies? Was it that the financially naïve bid up prices whilst the financially educated became caught up in the momentum and so altered their thinking to come into line with general opinion?

Le Bon had this to say:

"Because crowds possess these common ordinary qualities they can never accomplish acts demanding a high degree of intelligence — no matter how bright or knowledgeable some members may be, the crowd can only bring to bear in common the mediocre qualities of the average individual."

Or this, again from Le Bon:

"In a crowd every sentiment and act is contagious. And contagious to such a degree that an individual readily sacrifices his personal interest to the collective interest."

Le Bon is providing an explanation as to why even the professionals, the market economists and analysts, fall prey to the vagaries of mass market psychology. Why analysts place unrealistic values on loss making start-ups and why experienced economists predict more of the same despite the existence of inflated market pricing. Whilst they possess market knowledge it must not be forgotten that they are also human and so are subject to the same emotional influences.

Why is it that we conform to the consensus? Why is it rare for an individual to stand alone and express an independent and considered view? Why do we gain comfort in making our choice by viewing the actions of those around us? Why do we follow the crowd? Since it is so widespread it leads to the conclusion that this behaviour is innate. You must never forget that homo sapiens is part of the animal kingdom. Despite man's superior cognitive skills over those of the other animal species, his deep seated need to conform is, like other animals, inbuilt and automatic. It is most likely programmed as a survival instinct. A lovely quote on this behaviour is made by Justyn Walsh in his book *The Keynes Mutiny*.

"The caveman who — on seeing a torrent of people rushing past him, their faces contorted in a rictus of fear — declines to join the stampede is unlikely to have passed his genes on to posterity."[30]

Psychologist Solomon Asch conducted a study on social conformity in 1952. Groups comprising seven to nine individuals were coached to provide incorrect answers to simple questions with obvious answers. An unknowing experimental subject was then brought into the group. Twelve simple questions were asked to which the trained group provided unanimously incorrect answers. Despite the obvious nature of the correct answer, the experimental subject on a third of occasions also provided the wrong answer.

A variation of Asch's study was performed by Deutsch and Gerrard in 1955. Whilst Asch had the experimental subject provide answers within a group setting, Deutsch and Gerrard wanted to eradicate the possibility of peer group pressure in shaping the answer. Therefore, in their study, they allowed the experimental subject to provide his answer in an anonymous setting. The individual would, however, view a group response before answering. The experimental subject still provided the incorrect answer in approximately one out of every three answers.

The tendency for group thinking to influence an individual's decisions within the context of the financial markets is even greater than that seen in the aforementioned experiments. In Asch and Deutsch and Gerrard's studies the answers were obvious. In the financial markets they aren't. In an environment of uncertainty there is a greater temptation to accept what you are being told. For this very reason the investor is best warned against attending "investment clubs". These groups typically meet on a regular basis to discuss potential stock investments. Round table discussion occurs between amateur investors as a preliminary to committing a portion of pooled money. Attendees tend to gain comfort in their stock selections from group interaction and consensus but for all the reasons already discussed this is fraught with danger. It is not surprising that the number of these groups grows during bull markets at times when public interest in the stock market is heightened.

If even the experts advise that imprecision is the norm in the process of stock valuation, then is it no surprise that the novice looks to the crowd for the answers. Nor is it any surprise that the financial analyst who has based his decision on imprecise calculation can be swayed by the prevailing body of opinion. A professional may possess the skills of analysis but the tendency to conform is an emotional not an intellectual process. Many market professionals are not immune from group think.

A brief diversion away from the financial markets will reinforce how we can drop into group think without even being aware that it has occurred. Consider the true story of William Buckley, an English convict who was shipped out to Australia as a member of the first European settlement in Victoria. The settlement was established in 1803 when 400 settlers from England sailed into Port Phillip Bay aboard two ships, the "HMS Calcutta", a 52 gun man-o-war, and the "Ocean", a transport ship. William Buckley, then aged 23 years, was one of the 299 convicts who made up the party. Buckley, dissatisfied with settlement life, escaped into the Australian bush. When he later saw the ships pull up anchor and sail out of the bay (they were sailing to Tasmania to establish a settlement in Hobart), he knew he was now the sole European left on the shores of Port Phillip Bay. He spent the next 32 years living with the aborigines, most of the time was spent with the Barabool, a small group of the Wathaurong tribe around the Barwon River district. Buckley's next contact with Europeans was in 1835 when he was "discovered" by a European survey party. He was adopted back into European society where he remained until his death in 1856. His biography, written by John Morgan, was published in 1852. What is extraordinary about Buckley's story is that when he was found in 1835, after 32 years of cohabitation with the aborigines, he had totally adopted the aboriginal culture. He thought, behaved and spoke as an aboriginal. He had to relearn the English language despite having spent his first 23 years as an Englishman. That a mind can totally adapt to changes in its surroundings, that it can totally reconstruct its values and beliefs, was no less a surprise to Buckley himself. The following are his own words:

"The reader may wonder, how it was possible for anyone like myself who had, in my earlier life, been associated with civilised beings, so to live; but

I beg him to remember how many years I had led a different sort of existence, and how easy it is for the human being, as well as every other, to change his habits, taste, and may I add, feelings, when made the mere creator of circumstances. I look back now to that period of my life with inexpressible astonishment, considering it, as it were, altogether a dreaming delusion, and not reality."[31]

Buckley's mind had been totally "reprogrammed" to suit his new set of circumstances.

If we accept our susceptibility to group thought, if we are able to admit that our vulnerability is so pervasive that most will fall prey to it without even being aware of it happening, then we can begin to understand that those who can maintain an independence of mind will have the greatest chance of investment success. You should be seeking correctness not consensus.

The Greek philosopher Socrates (470 BC–399 BC) defined the framework for what is now termed Socratic Method. Socratic Method tells us that the correctness of a statement cannot be determined by whether it is held by the majority, rather that it is incapable of being rationally contradicted. By the use of the Socratic Method you need not second-guess whether the majority is correct or not. Simply ignore the crowd and determine for yourself what is the correct (or as near as possible to correct) answer. There is no doubt that Ben Graham adopted Socratic Method in his approach to market analysis. He clearly articulated this in his book *The Intelligent Investor*:

"You are neither right nor wrong because the crowd disagrees with you. You are right because your data and reasoning are right."[32]

In order to achieve success you must, as Warren Buffett has told us, possess a "sound intellectual framework for making decisions and the ability to keep emotions from corroding that framework."

CHAPTER 16

Misperceptions

*"The investor's chief problem — and even his
worst enemy — is likely to be himself."*

BEN GRAHAM

There are two principal routes to an education. One is to learn the correct answers from the outset and the other is to dive into the process and then by trial and error reject that which doesn't work and retain that which does. Unfortunately if you base your financial education solely on the latter technique then much of your time will be spent losing money rather than building a capital base of any magnitude. Much of a financial education should be formed by learning from the mistakes of others before you have the opportunity to make them yourself. Of course there does ultimately come a time when you need to take a position in the market and there is no doubt that the education process continues on from there. When mistakes are made, as they invariably will be, you must learn by them and not go on to repeat them. Unfortunately too many people enter the market ill-prepared for the task. They have neither developed the intellectual framework from which to make investment decisions nor are they aware of the multitude of misjudgments that they have the potential to make.

The novice investor, or indeed the unsuccessful investor who has failed to interpret the reasons behind his failures, should be aware of the nature of these potential misjudgments. That incorrect decisions are made by a great many investors needs to be an accepted fact. As Fred Kelly stated in his 1930 book *Why You Win or Lose — The Psychology of Speculation*:

"Every natural human impulse seems to be a foe to success in stocks."[33]

It's these impulses that tell us to sell in depressed markets and buy in inflated markets. It's why we base our decisions on hope rather than fact. And it's why we justify our decisions by accepting only that information which confirms them and putting little weight on that which doesn't. In order to achieve superior investment performance our thinking and our emotions must not guide us into making the same mistakes as those made by the general investment population. We must excel rather than follow if we hope to outperform.

To assist in understanding what needs to be done in order to achieve better than average returns (i.e. to "beat the market") then consider the total value of all the companies which are listed on a particular stock exchange as representing a single measurable pool. From that pool flows a quantifiable investment return which is available to all the investors who are holding stock in companies that make up that pool. Whether your return is larger or smaller than the next person is dependent not only on how much money you have invested in the pool but also upon how you have allocated your capital (i.e. which companies you have invested your money in). If you have invested well and in companies with above average returns then your overall return will exceed the market average. A result of you receiving a higher than average return is that there is less for distribution to other investors who must therefore receive a below average return. For this to occur consistently you must be "smarter than the pack". An integral part of being smarter than the pack is not to make the same mistakes that others will almost certainly be making. The following discussion outlines some of the principal misjudgments that you can fall prey to. If these misjudgments are not heeded then your returns will suffer.

UNREALISTIC EXPECTATIONS

Perhaps the first and most fundamental mistake that the novice investor will make is one of unrealistic expectations. He feels that every market position taken will result in a positive outcome. If an investor's initial investments are made during the course of a bull market then this misperception is likely to be reinforced. However, in a volatile market or a bear market it is unlikely to be long before current market prices have fallen below the investor's entry prices hence presenting a paper loss. This is often interpreted as a failure. Why? Because the misperception is held that successful investors don't ever lose. This expectation should be relegated to the same area as the expectation of a visit from Father Christmas or the Easter Bunny.

The successful investor expects failures but has an understanding of how to manage the situation. He has a handle on the risks before an investment position is even taken. He appreciates the possible outcome of his actions and that one of these possible outcomes is that the market price of a stockholding can decline. An inability to act appropriately when these circumstances are faced is a more valid determinant of investment failure than the simple fact that the price of the stock has fallen.

It is important to stress that successful investors are not infallible. They all make investment decisions that they later regret. The difference is that successful investors make fewer mistakes and when they do occur a strategy has already been formulated to minimise their negative impact. Read on.

FALSE PREDICTIONS

The framework of knowledge upon which an experienced investor bases his decisions takes time and effort to develop. But the novice investor has usually devoted little by way of time or effort to developing his own intellectual framework. Therefore he lacks the capacity to develop his own investment strategies. In a full blown bull market this usually doesn't matter. Novice investors are likely to boldly enter the market having gained confidence from the actions of those around them. At times when the bull isn't roaring the confidence to make investment decisions is harder to find. They must look to others to call the shots for them. Therefore they turn to the so-called "market experts". Herein lies the second fallacy — that "market experts" can predict the future.

We are constantly being presented with the opinions of market commentators in the newspapers and on the TV. But the operative word is opinion. Unfortunately the public eye can cause experts to lose their sense of humility. They start to express their opinion with such a degree of confidence that it is misinterpreted by the unknowing as fact. Being put upon a pedestal and declared to be an expert carries with it an expectation that the expert has an insight that everyone else is lacking. An expert can't afford to be imprecise. An expert usually lacks the humility to admit that he doesn't know the answer. An opinion must always be expressed and it must always be delivered with an air of authority that many misinterpret to carry the weight of certainty. This is particularly dangerous when "experts" start predicting the future. Economists seem to love this game. Typically they are well dressed, well educated and express their views using terminology that befits the public's expectation that they know the answers. It must be strongly stated that no-one has yet provided any evidence of a capacity to predict the future direction of the stock market.

It has been said that there are three kinds of investors:

1 Investors who don't know what the market will do and know they don't know.
2 Investors who don't know what the market will do but don't know that they don't know.
3 Investors who don't know what the market will do but get paid a lot of money to pretend they know.

Unfortunately a large proportion of people are included in group two and too many people are influenced by those that fall into group three.

These comments relate to market movements within cycles because the fact is that if you have a time frame that is long enough the direction of the market is predictable. That's because the long term trend has always been up. But where people get unstuck is when their investment time line falls foul of the market cycle. On occasions the market cycle has been a very long one. As an example of how long it can be consider what happened following the famous 1929 crash. In its aftermath the US stock market finally bottomed in 1932 but it wasn't until 1954 that it regained the level seen just before the crash. Fortunately most recoveries don't take anywhere near this long. By way of example the average period for recovery to pre crash levels following the last nine Australian bear markets has been 41 months.

The trick is not to overpay for stocks at any stage of the cycle. The successful investor needs to have an appreciation of value — that what they are buying is in fact worth what they are paying for it. Value can be found at any time in the market cycle but is just more prevalent at times when prices are generally depressed. Peter Lynch, successful past manager of the Fidelity Magellan Fund, had this to say of market timing (i.e. attempts at profiting from predicting the short to medium term future direction of the market):

> "I'd love to be able to predict markets and anticipate recessions, but since that's impossible, I'm as satisfied to search out profitable companies as Buffett is."

And Warren Buffett himself had this to say:

> "I am not in the business of predicting general stock market or business fluctuations. If you think I can do this, or think it's essential to an investment program, you should not be in the partnership."[34]

And Buffett again in 1987:

> "I have never met a man who could forecast the market."[35]

OVERCONFIDENCE

A survey in Sweden showed that 90 per cent of drivers considered themselves above average. In another study, researcher James Montier found that of 300 professional fund managers surveyed 74 per cent of them felt that they had delivered above average job performance. The remaining 26 per cent saw themselves as having demonstrated average performance!

There is a tendency for us to overestimate our capabilities. This is no less so in the financial arena than in any other of life's endeavours. There is a natural tendency for investors to credit their success during a bull market phase to their own stock picking skills. Yet when the general market moves against them they tend to blame their losses on either poor advice or adverse market movements. This fact was highlighted in a 1998 *Wall Street Journal* article which was reporting the results of a poll taken by the Gallup organisation:

"As stock prices hover at or near records, a new poll indicates that inexperienced investors expect considerably higher returns on their portfolios than do long time investors — and are more confident of their ability to beat the market".

There is also a tendency for people to confuse familiarity with knowledge. Ask a group of people if they know what the Dow Jones Index is. Watch for the large number of affirmative replies. Ask now how it is calculated and what information it provides. Be prepared for the silence. Everyone has heard the words but few can actually provide any meaningful explanation of what the words mean. Numerous other examples exist. Just as everyone thinks they are a good driver so too do they think they are a good investor.

And remember this: when you are buying someone else is selling. What makes you so sure that the person selling the stock is the one who is making the wrong decision?

ILLUSION OF CONTROL

Consider the thought processes associated with the purchase of a lottery ticket. Often those who choose their own numbers feel that they have a better chance of winning than if their numbers were randomly selected. Or consider the fact that some people feel more willing to bet on the outcome of a coin toss if they can make their call before the toss rather than after it has occurred. This behaviour is illogical but common.

Often investors feel that they are in control of an investment situation when in reality they aren't. This is particularly true of investor behaviour in a bull market and has led to the saying "Don't confuse brains with a bull market".

During the course of a rising stock market the novice investor often makes many buy and sell decisions. The general uptrend of stock prices shields him from the reality that his decisions are not necessarily improving his returns. All he sees is his portfolio balance rising. But there is a very high probability that this would have occurred if he had simply bought stock and held it. He draws the wrong conclusion that it is his activity which has made the difference. The reality is that few investors possess the skills that allow their decisions to influence the outcome. If you genuinely wish to get to this stage then there is still a lot of work ahead.

OVER-REACTION TO RECENT NEWS

The present value of a share, in theory, should be equivalent to the total value of all future cash flows which ownership bestows, after having adjusted each to allow for risk and the time value of money (by applying an appropriate discount rate). The problem is of course that no-one knows what these future cash flows are going to be. Because future events are unknown current circumstances predominate in shaping opinions and in forming estimates regarding future company earnings, dividend rates and growth prospects. The mistake is that the future performance of the company is not determined solely by what is happening at that particular point in time. This short-sightedness stems partly from the fact that current events at least present something that is concrete, something on which current investment decisions can be pinned and partly from the influence of the prevailing mood and the influence of group think.

Sure an outbreak of equine flu can affect the profitability of a company which has a revenue stream that depends on the horse racing industry. However, its stock price need not be decimated upon news of the outbreak. Flu epidemics are transient. Hopefully the company isn't. The same can be said of the effect of a builders' labourers' strike on construction stocks or that of a cyclical drop in base metal prices on mining stocks. Markets tend to overshoot on the news. Since the market typically prices long term assets with a short term focus opportunities exist for those investors who can recognise short term mispricing and are prepared to take a long term view. But be careful. This activity should be limited to those companies which are financially sound and are suffering what is likely to be only a temporary setback.

The words of Ben Graham are particularly relevant to the act of purchasing companies which have been sold off on recent news:

> "The investor would need more than a mere falling off in both earnings and price to give him a sound basis for purchase. He should require an indication of at least reasonable stability of earnings over the past decade or more — i.e. no year of earnings deficit — plus sufficient size and financial strength to meet possible setbacks in the future."

OVERTRADING

The difference between a trader (speculator) and an investor has already been discussed. The trader buys stock in the hope that it will be on sold for a higher price. The investor purchases stock for a price which he anticipates will be exceeded by the discounted value of future cash flows. To the investor, however, those future cash flows are not represented purely by capital gain. Dividends become an important component of future returns. In explaining the difference, John Maynard Keynes distinguished between what he saw as exchange values and ultimate values.

All too often novice investors fail to recognise the distinction. They perceive themselves to be investors but in reality behave as traders. They purchase and sell stocks so often that it approaches the regularity that they change their clothes. They consider that activity in the market is a necessary part of investment. True investors might be active but it doesn't necessarily mean that they are buying or selling. They are more likely to be devoting their energy to monitoring existing holdings and attempting to identify further investment opportunities. If the retention of existing holdings is warranted and further investment opportunities cannot be found, then inactivity is the appropriate behaviour.

Warren Buffett has described his favourite holding period as forever. Brilliant American engineer and mathematician Claude Shannon possessed the same sentiment towards his investment portfolio. Shannon is recognised for his development of the digital circuit design which ultimately formed the basis of modern computers. But despite his strong interest in developing computers Shannon also devoted significant time to the investment process. Measured over a 35 year investment period he achieved an annual growth rate on his holdings of 28 per cent, far exceeding that of the general indices. Shannon didn't trade. His principal stocks were bought and held for decades. This example of course doesn't provide statistical proof that those actions, if emulated will provide the same result. It is, however, an interesting demonstration that activity is not a necessary component of success. In fact, as the following discussion demonstrates, activity can seriously undermine returns due to the effect of taxes and transaction costs.

What any investor must remember is that success in their activity is achieved by the appropriate allocation of capital. They should not misinterpret their activity of buying and selling as income generating activity. It is the brokers who receive income as a result of the activity of buying and selling. Investors must remember that they are buying part ownership of a company. It is the activities of the company itself which will generate the investor's income. The investor has allocated the capital — job done. The income flows from the activity of the management and workers of the company the stock of which has been purchased.

Trading, or the regular turnover of stock, can result in a negative impact on returns as a result of the not so insignificant costs of transaction fees and capital gains taxes. Consider the following which would be applicable to Australian taxpayers. In order to keep the example simple the impact of capital gains taxes alone are considered.

Investor A makes an initial investment of $10,000 for a 20 year period. He sells his holding and reinvests in new stocks twice a year. Assume for the purpose of discussion the highest marginal tax rate and a 12 per cent average annual capital gain. His cash return after 20 years is slightly in excess of $34,000. Investor B makes the same initial investment of $10,000 but maintains his portfolio for 20 years and then converts it to cash. He too pays capital gains tax but only once at the end of the 20 year period. Investor B ends up holding $76,000 at the end of the 20 year period, double that of Investor A. Same initial capital, same annual return of 12 per cent. The difference is due totally to the impact of capital gains taxes. The assumption here is that the trader has regularly changed his position in an attempt to chase better investment returns.

Three points need to be made however. Firstly the question needs to be asked whether he is changing his holding to better yielding stocks or is he in fact changing on the basis of a whim or a desire to simply be active in the market? Secondly if he is changing his holding on the basis of new analysis, then you have to seriously question his stock picking skill since none are being held for any length of time. And thirdly even if he has the ability to select stocks that outperform the general market, then they will have to do so by a significant margin so as to make up for the erosive nature of transaction fees and capital gains taxes.

Having said that, do not take the preceding discussion as a blanket argument against trading. Successful traders do exist but it is important to note that these are people who have developed significant skill in what they do. If you don't possess these skills then the risks of losing money are high. Seasoned traders don't simply buy and sell and so automatically generate an income. They are represented by a group of disciplined operators who understand the risks associated with the positions they take and what to do when things go wrong. It is a commonly quoted statistic that 90 per cent of people who undertake the activity of trading lose money. It would be wrong to assume that you wouldn't be included in this number.

GAMBLER'S FALLACY

Reference has already been made to Warren Buffett's talk given at Columbia University in 1984 when he proposed a hypothetical coin flipping contest involving 225 million Americans. If each initially wagered a dollar and then engaged in an instant death playoff whereby they put up their entire kitty each day, it would be found that within four weeks time there would be a single person holding the total $225 million. The winner would have made a successful coin toss on every day of the contest. Yet consider what would have been going through the mind of that person on each day. On the first day the winner would have expected a 50:50 chance of success. But as each day proceeded thoughts such as "My luck is about to run out" or "It's been heads four times in a row now, it's time for tails," would have entered the winner's mind. For most people in this situation there would be a growing expectation that the outcome is due to fall against them. This is because the expectation is for an equal number of heads and tails to fall. As each successive toss results in a head the expectation grows that a tail will fall next. But the reality is that the outcome of the last coin toss has no bearing on the chance of the next toss resulting in either a head or a tail. A biased expectation formed from the observation of the outcomes of past chance events is referred to as Gambler's Fallacy.

Swiss mathematician Jacob Bernoulli propounded the "Golden Theorem" later known as the "Law of Large Numbers" in a 1713 paper on probability. He proposed that for a sample of independent variables it is the average of these observations that will eventually approach the expected value not the actual number itself. So if a coin is tossed one million times it is unlikely to fall heads 500,000 times. In fact as the number of tosses increases, it is to be expected that the difference between the actual number of heads and the actual number of tails increases. It is the ratio of heads to tails that more closely approaches the expectation, i.e. a ratio of 50:50. There is a world of difference between the two. The law of large numbers helps explain why it is wrong to use a ratio or an expected probability in an attempt to accurately predict a near term outcome. If the stock market has traditionally had a down year one in four and the last three years have shown positive returns, that does not mean that next year will be a down year. This law can also be applied to the consideration of expected market returns. Professor Jeremy Siegel tells us that the US stock market has provided an above inflation return (dividends reinvested) of 7 per cent over the period from 1802 to 1997. This does not mean that your portfolio will provide you with a 7 per cent return next year or even the year after. Nor does it mean that if you receive a 14 per cent return this year then you are likely to receive a zero per cent return next. What it does mean is that your chances of receiving a return approximating the long term average will increase the longer that you hold your stock portfolio. Gambler's Fallacy is to apply long term averages to short term horizons.

FALLING IN LOVE WITH A STOCK

Some investors buy a stock and expect, from that point in time, that the stock will rise in value. The company might have been in business for 50 or 100 years before the investor showed any interest in it but now that he has purchased its stock, he expects the price will soar. In keeping with this expectation, he eagerly refers to the newspaper or internet daily to check the quoted price. It's as if the entire market was holding back the stock price until he got on board. Fred Kelly, author of *Why You Win or Lose — The Psychology of Speculation*, dedicated a chapter of his book to this behaviour which he termed "Perils of the Will to Believe".[36]

The simple reality is that a stock will not increase in price nor will it be a superior investment simply because you own it. Coupled with this ill-founded belief is the tendency to "fall in love" with a stock. This arises when a stock is purchased with high expectations but it fails to deliver. Nevertheless the stock continues to be held because the investor has developed an attachment to it. It might have a nice sounding name or manufacture a product that he likes. Alternatively it might be the first stock he ever purchased. Despite there being a legitimate reason for selling the stock he hangs on because he has an emotional attachment to it. Emotion clouds judgment.

LIVING IN HOPE

For the skilled stock picker, the individual who is confident in his ability to make a relatively good assessment of fair value, a falling stock price might not be a concern. He has a strength of conviction and a faith in his own skills of valuation that allow him to judge the stock as representing good value despite the change in sentiment against it. But note the reference to "skilled stock picker". You won't find one on every street corner. For the overwhelming majority, skills in valuation are limited. The quoted stock price is relied upon as the surrogate assessment of value. Consequently a falling stock price presents them with a dilemma. They don't know whether to sell the stock on the chance that the price will fall further or to hold it in the hope that its price will turn around. Many resolve this dilemma by telling themselves that they will sell when the stock rises back to the entry price, that is the price which they originally paid for it. That way they won't have to admit to having made a loss. This behaviour has been termed the Disposition Effect, a phrase coined by Hersch Shefrin and Meir Statman in 1985. It is the pre*disposition* to get evenitis.

The simple fact is that people can live in hope all they want but if the lower price is justified on the basis of new information then hope will not change anything. A seasoned investor will decide whether to continue holding the stock based on what rule or set of investment principles he already had in place were this situation to arise. That is, he knows beforehand what he would do if the stock price were to fall. The rules that guide action vary from investor to investor but nevertheless they are in place and have been established on the basis of considered analysis undertaken well before they need to be applied.

For an investor to continue holding a stock solely because he hopes it will return to the entry price proves that he either has yet to derive or is failing to act upon a set of solid investment principles.

SELLING TOO EARLY

In addition to the tendency to hold onto losers, there is tendency to sell winners too early. Legendary investor Peter Lynch described this behaviour as watering the weeds and cutting the flowers. Fred Kelly feels that it is vanity that leads us to take small profits but endure large losses. He believes that selling a stock for a price greater than for which it was purchased is a "sop to vanity" and that no matter how small that advance may have been it is perceived as demonstrating an ability to beat the market. However, to sell a stock that has lost ground since being purchased would be an admission of failure and hence not willingly accepted.

Terrance Odean examined trades associated with 10,000 accounts from a US broking house to see whether investors do actually tend to water the weeds and cut the flowers when it comes to making investment decisions.[37] He found that, on average, the stocks which had gone up in value but were sold outperformed the market by 2.35 per cent over the following 12 months. He also found that stocks which had experienced a price decline but were held went on to underperform the market by 1.06 per cent over the following 12 months. Whilst these may appear to be small percentages they certainly aren't. Alterations to returns of this magnitude can have a profound effect on portfolio returns over time. A professional portfolio manager would forego his next Christmas bonus in order to achieve this sort of boost to his investment returns.

IMPATIENCE

It has been stated that Professor Jeremy Siegel calculated that from 1802 to 1997 the compound annual real rate of return for US stocks was 7 per cent.[38] Real return is the return after the rate of inflation has been deducted. This figure of 7 per cent doesn't simply reflect capital gains but takes into consideration reinvestment of dividends.

This reinvestment provides a significant boost to overall returns. Siegel tells us that if reinvestment of dividends is not included in the calculation then the real capital appreciation over the same period was 1.6 per cent. The figure is higher if the nineteenth century is excluded. For the period 1926 to 1997 it was 2.8 per cent and this figure is higher again if only the latter part of the twentieth century is considered. Therefore it can be seen that general price growth, as measured by appreciation in general stock indices, is relatively modest when measured over extended periods of time. This is not to deny that stocks represent an outstanding investment, rather to remind the reader that this is a race that is typically won over an extended period. Of course the race speed varies. Sometimes it's a sprint, sometimes the runner is asleep and sometimes he is running backwards. But taken over the long term progress is in a forward direction.

Let's consider at what speed the race would need to be run if it proceeded at a constant pace. That is, if there were no market fluctuations. Stock prices neither fell nor stagnated. They advanced every day. Under this scenario the investor who checks the daily price of his holdings would always be satisfied that his stocks had in fact advanced. But by how much would they have advanced? Let's hypothetically propose, for the purpose of the example, that the nominal annual rate (real rate plus inflation) of stock price advance is 6 per cent. This is not an unrealistic proposal and certainly within the realms of what has occurred historically. In order to satisfy this linear advance, a 30¢ stock would need to increase in price by one 140th of a cent on each reported trading day during the course of the first year. In other words, the eager stockholder would open up the newspaper after each trading day to find that the price of his 30¢ stock had advanced by one 140th of a cent on the day. Of course this is ridiculous but the point should be taken. In the real world stocks regularly rise and regularly fall in price. This is normal price behaviour. True and lasting advances must be viewed over a much longer time frame than a day.

Let's approach the discussion from a slightly different direction. A one day rise of 1¢ in a 30¢ stock is a rise of greater than 3 per cent.

This is a substantial rise but as previously mentioned one that might be expected by the eager novice. However it would be unrealistic to expect a percentage rise of this magnitude to regularly occur. If you expected a 3 per cent rise every trading day then a single 30¢ stock would be valued at $1,163 in a year's time and at $4.5 million at the end of two years. It is more realistic to expect a 1¢ rise within a six month period. On a day-to-day basis you should no more expect a 1¢ rise in the price of a stock than a 1¢ fall.

Let's continue to put expectations at a realistic level. It is widely accepted within financial circles that Warren Buffett has established himself as the most successful investor of all time. In an investing career that has to date spanned over 50 years, he has accumulated a body of capital that has earned him the title as one of the wealthiest men in the world. He achieved this without any form of inheritance. By achieving high investment returns over an extended period of time he had by early 2010 compounded his modest seed capital into a personal fortune of $50 billion.

In checking his investment record we see that between 1956 and 1969 he achieved an average annual return of slightly less than 30 per cent. From 1969 to 2000 his average return was 24 per cent. These are extraordinarily high returns. The US market average return over the same period was 12 per cent. Twelve per cent is clearly closer to what the average investor could have expected over the same period. This is not consistent with expectations of doubling your money within short time frames. Indeed Warren Buffett doesn't expect to double his money overnight so why should you?

LOWER PRICED STOCKS REPRESENT BETTER VALUE

This investor misperception reminds me of the story of the man who entered a restaurant and ordered a take-away pizza. Upon removing the freshly cooked pizza from the oven the restaurant owner asked the man whether he would prefer the pizza to be cut up into quarters or eighths. The man responded that he would prefer it to be divided into eight portions as he was feeling particularly hungry.

In a similar fashion stocks represent but a portion of a company. No matter how many ordinary shares are on offer the company remains the same size. If the market values a company at $100 million and there are 100 million ordinary shares in existence then each will trade at $1. If there are 10 million shares then they will be trading at $10. It is value that the investor should be focusing on, not price. In order to appreciate this each calculation must be company specific and relate the number of shares on issue to the value of the company as a whole. Yet despite this simple fact many investors believe that they are achieving better value by purchasing low priced offerings.

Running in total contrast to this thinking is US company Berkshire Hathaway. At the time of writing, its shares were trading in the order of $100,000 each. Ordinarily a company's management would have undertaken a stock split long before its stock price approached this sort of level. It is a commonly held belief that a lower price facilitates trade in a company's stock. Management often extols the benefits of liquidity whereby if the company has an active trade in its stock it allows prospective investors to easily acquire its stock and existing stockholders to easily sell.

Why then the stance taken by Berkshire Hathaway? Three reasons are put forward as to why they have resisted a stock split. Firstly they argue that high stock turnover is undesirable. A high stock turnover leads to an increase in transaction costs which lowers overall returns. Secondly Berkshire wishes to (and has achieved) a highly loyal and stable stockholder base. They see it as undesirable to attract stockholders with a short term market orientation. And thirdly as a result of the first two reasons they perceive there to be an increased tendency for market prices to depart materially from fair value. Why is the latter point undesirable? If market price and fair value are not aligned then this will produce situations when trade in that company's stock will favour some and disadvantage others. A seller is disadvantaged at times of a depressed stock price and a buyer is disadvantaged at times of an elevated stock price. You might say that there is an irony in that Warren Buffett, who is the manager of and principal stockholder in Berkshire, is not wanting the market price of Berkshire to stray from its fair value, since it is this principle of mispricing which has enabled him to amass a fortune. But remember that his duty as a custodian of other people's funds has been to optimise their capital and once so accumulated to protect it and to distribute it fairly.

As a final comment, Berkshire Hathaway did recognise that some of its stockholders found the high stock price to pose some difficulties. This was particularly so in terms of the imposition of US gift duties whereby a single unit of Berkshire Hathaway stock exceeded the threshold for the imposition of these duties. Consequently Class B stock was introduced in addition to the original (Class A) stock. A holder of Class A stock can convert any Class A share held into 30 Class B shares. However, the conversion cannot occur in the opposite direction. Appropriately the Class B shares trade at very close to one-thirtieth of the value of Class A shares.

ACTING ON INCOMPLETE INFORMATION

With the widespread adoption of the internet and cable TV our access to information has taken a quantum leap. The magnitude and ease of access to inputs for making investment decisions has not only grown exponentially but continues to rise. Despite this there remains significant doubt as to whether it has facilitated the investment process.

To most people, however, this doesn't present as a problem. As if to shield themselves from complex issues, they tend to base their decisions on a very small set of information and often on the wrong information altogether. This is not unique to decision-making in the financial arena. It is common to decision-making in general. It has been the subject of psychological study and accordingly identified behaviour patterns have been tagged with specific names.

Representativeness is a collective term used to describe a range of misperceptions people have when judging probabilities. Under the umbrella of representativeness is "Gambler's Fallacy" and the "Law of Large Numbers" which have already been discussed. Another important misperception which falls into this group is an insensitivity to the probability of outcomes. Or put another way, it is the failure to recognise that common things occur commonly. An example might be the response given to the following. You meet someone for the first time. He is youthful, small, has a high pitched voice and an attractive wife. He wears jewellery and drives an expensive car. Is he more likely to be a jockey or a labourer? The tendency is to answer jockey since the description better fits the stereotype. However, the fact is that there are many more labourers than there are jockeys and this should carry significant weight in the analysis. A shortcut or rule of thumb of this type has been described by US psychologists Amos Tversky and Daniel Kahneman as a representativeness heuristic.

Representativeness therefore can lead us to a tendency to make poor judgments because we are discarding important facts in an attempt to fast-track our decision-making based on prior experience. We are making the dual mistakes of ignoring what is potentially important information and placing too much weight on the limited information that we choose to use. Notable cognitive psychologist and computer scientist Herbert Simon was, amongst many other interests, a pioneer in the field of artificial intelligence and a theorist on how humans learn. The following statement is attributed to him:

"What information consumes is rather obvious: it consumes the attention of its recipients. Hence a wealth of information creates a poverty of attention, and a need to allocate that attention efficiently among the overabundance of information sources that might consume it."[39]

Simon felt that we react to only a small part of the information which is available to us. Since we don't draw conclusions from the full set of information there is no guarantee that the information which we do use is representative of the entire set. This increases our chances of deriving an answer that is wrong.

Whilst Simon did significant work in this area the concept of acting on incomplete information was not a new one. These quotes from G.C. Seldon's 1912 book entitled *The Psychology of the Stock Market* highlight this fact:

"Every human mind has its own peculiarities, so presumably yours has, though you can't see them plainly..."[40]

And further:

"However important some single factor in the situation may appear to you, it is not going to control the movement of prices regardless of everything else."[41]

If we are using information that has been drawn from an incomplete data set there remains the possibility that it approximates the complete data set. But if we then consciously and specifically select information we are introducing strong personal biases. It's as if we have derived the answer before reviewing the information and then only selected that information which confirms what we want to believe. Called confirmation bias, it is a very common form of human behaviour. Consider a patient who attends a doctor's surgery seeking both a diagnosis and cure for a set of symptoms. If the patient finds the treatment offered by the first doctor to be distasteful it is possible that he will seek a second opinion. He is hopeful that the second doctor will offer what often amounts to a less invasive treatment. If he finds a doctor who will deliver the treatment he prefers then he is more likely to condemn the first doctor as incompetent. People tend to believe what they want to believe. They accept evidence that confirms their beliefs and reject that which doesn't. Beliefs which are formed from unsound reasoning are dangerous ones to hold.

Random reinforcement is another phenomenon which causes people to behave illogically. It is often the cause of gambling addictions. It has encouraged day traders to continue trading until all funds are exhausted. It was quite likely a contributing factor to the downfall of the hedge fund, Long Term Capital Management, which was discussed in chapter 13. Random reinforcement describes the reinforcement of our behaviour, by way of either positive or negative outcomes, but where that reinforcement is inconsistent in nature. From a very young age we have been conditioned by relatively consistent feedback. Good behaviour has been encouraged by positive feedback and bad behaviour by negative. By this method we learn by correcting our behaviour to maximise reward and minimise adverse outcomes. Financial markets, however, present price behaviour that tends to be inconsistent. Prices can move up or down in the short to medium term, reversing direction in a manic pattern. Therefore over a similar time frame an investment can be rewarded or punished by a market that is insensitive to the actions of those who have recently allocated their capital to it.

How then do we react to this inconsistency? Faced with failure we remember the success and expect future success to reverse the effect of adverse events and outcomes. Gamblers do sometimes win and it is the memory of these wins that keeps them going during periods of loss. For some the danger is that it keeps them going for a period that is long enough to take them to financial ruin. When an investor begins to behave as a gambler, he ceases to be an investor. As stated earlier emotion corrupts rational thought and it is rational thought that must be undertaken by anyone who hopes to succeed as an investor.

LIMITATIONS ASSOCIATED WITH INFORMATION PROCESSING

One of the greatest barriers to our ability to successfully analyse a stock's prospects might lie in the way our brains process information. In order to explore this concept further consider the task that confronts the investment analyst or would be investor. His aim is to purchase an asset. In the case of this discussion that asset is stock which will provide future inflation and risk adjusted cash flows exceeding the amount initially outlaid to purchase it. The higher these future cash flows the better. To do this our analyst analyses the prospects of the alternative investments on offer. He could consider an enormous number of inputs that have the potential to impact on the future profitability of each company under consideration. The size and scope of this list is nearly endless. These inputs can be considered at three principal levels: at the level of the general economy, at the industry sector level or at the company specific level. They cover the spectrum from macro to micro. They can include just about anything from a change of management to the chance of World War III commencing. Not only is the analyst attempting to quantify the financial impact of these inputs on the stock price but the reality is that because he is dealing with predicting future events he doesn't actually know which of them will occur and which won't.

Here is where the process gets really messy. Not only does the analyst have to deal with an almost boundless information set, not only does he attempt to predict the future, and not only does he attempt to quantify the financial impact of that which is unpredictable and unquantifiable but he has to do it better than the next guy. Being a successful investor is not about being as "correct" as everyone else. It is about recognising things that others haven't. Because if it has already been widely considered the chances are that it is already reflected in the stock price.

What if the analyst is told what is going to happen in the future? Not what the stock price is going to be but what the variables which are likely to influence the stock price are going to be. What if he has a crystal ball? Would this mean that he could calculate a future stock price? The most likely answer is no. The problem lies in the way our brains process information. The human brain tends to process information in a linear or sequential manner. Given the change in a single variable (a pricing input) we seem to be able to estimate its impact on the outcome (the price). But the world of financial analysis is not so simple. There are a multitude of inputs that have the potential to impact on the stock price. And as each changes it has a variable impact on a multitude of other inputs which in turn impact in a variety of ways on all the others. There is a complex multiplicity of negative and positive feedback loops interconnected in a three-dimensional web that would make even the most sophisticated modern day computer blow a fuse. The human brain is just not wired to perform at this level. Many sophisticated investors recognise this fact and therefore limit the inputs they use for investment decision-making. Not only do they use fewer inputs but they look for the ones that they feel are likely to have the biggest impact on future cash flows. This has led to the common observation that more information doesn't always lead to better investment results.

Information processing that allows for the positive or negative adjustment of a variable within a three-dimensional feedback system is called interactive or configurable processing. Studies have looked at our capacity to process information in this manner. Paul Slovic, Professor of Psychology at the University of Oregon, specifically tested stock market professionals in order to measure to what degree they used interactive processing in the stock selection process. In one study Slovic provided thirteen stockbrokers and five finance graduate students with eight simple financial inputs. They were asked to use interactive thinking in making investment decisions. In evaluating the test data Slovic used a statistical test called an ANOVA test (analysis of variance test) which attempts to explain observed differences between groups or populations. His results demonstrated that interactive thinking accounted for only about four per cent of the decisions that were made. What's more Slovic found that there was a discrepancy between how test participants actually processed the information and what they reported to be their method of processing the information. This was particularly so of the experienced brokers. In fact the more experienced the broker the greater was the tendency for a discrepancy to exist between the actual and the reported method of analysis. It was as if they were aware of the required method but were unable or unprepared to undertake it. Maybe with experience comes a growing realisation of an incapacity to undertake analysis at this level.

These findings are not unique to financial analysts. It is a human characteristic not a professional one. Similar decision-making processes are undertaken by professionals in other fields. Therefore it is no surprise that financial analysis, particularly that which attempts to predict the specific price of a stock in the future, can be found lacking when we acknowledge that we:

1 Introduce bias when selecting the information used in the process of analysis.
2 Are only capable of processing the information in a very basic way.
3 Rely on information that time will most likely prove to be wrong.

It is an important step for the budding market participant to become aware of both his limited ability to process information and potential emotional weaknesses. Experienced traders and investors are acutely aware of how counter-productive emotional issues can be and that their best chance of negating their erosive effect is to utilise techniques that minimise or exclude them from the decision-making process. Seasoned players establish a set of mechanical rules that govern their decision-making. A common example is the stop loss order which guards against traders or investors living in hope that a stock which has fallen in price will recover to the entry level (when the risk is that it could continue to fall in price). And it is why value investors such as David Dreman[42] and James O'Shaughnessy[43] advocate the use of objectivity-based screening mechanisms when selecting value stocks. Disciplined market participants have defined certain parameters that a stock must fulfil before being bought and they know what circumstances will trigger its sale. Whilst we can never expect to process information like robots mechanical rules can at least protect us from our worst enemy — ourselves.

CHAPTER 17

Volatility and risk aren't synonymous

"Unless you can watch your stockholding decline by 50 per cent without becoming panic stricken, you should not be in the stock market."

WARREN BUFFETT

How often do you hear someone state that he perceives the stock market as risky? Then in an effort to substantiate his statement he confidently tells you by how much the market value of shares fluctuates from month to month and year to year. He doesn't realise it but he is admitting that he doesn't actually understand what risk means. What he is doing is confusing risk with volatility. There is a substantial difference between the two. Understanding this difference is so fundamental to investment success that it is appropriate to devote an entire chapter to explaining it.

It has been stated that ignorance and fear are a dangerous combination to bring to the financial markets. But of course the two are inter-related as is indicated by the expression "Fear of the Unknown". Knowledge is often the antidote for fear. Indeed the first thing done to alleviate a child's fear of the dark is to turn on the lights so as to demonstrate that there is nothing sinister lurking in the room. Hence it is important that any would-be investor undertakes a financial education. Even if you choose not to develop your knowledge to the level whereby you can select individual stocks, an understanding of how markets move should be undertaken as a bare minimum.

Even if you choose to abrogate the stock selection decision and invest your money in a managed or index fund, you will still be open to the vagaries of general market movement. The price of units in managed or index funds fluctuates in accordance with the market price of their combined parts. Consequently the holders of units in a diversified fund will see the value of their investment swing in a similar manner to the general market.

An understanding of how the general market moves is a good place to start an investment education. Any investor who contemplates purchasing stocks, bonds, real estate or any financial product which is based on these assets should understand how the prices of these can fluctuate. To understand what actually causes them to move provides an interesting intellectual exercise but doesn't need to be where the financial education starts. What is essential basic knowledge is to appreciate the magnitude and timing through which markets can move. This distinction is encompassed in the saying:

"It is not necessary to know what moves markets, rather how markets move."

Indeed what moves markets is not totally understood. This was summed up in the following quote by James Palysted Wood:

"The thing that most affects the stock market is everything."

Factors such as economic growth, interest rates and business, consumer and investor confidence are all considered to be important factors. But many of these are difficult to measure and their exact interplay is unclear. Therefore it is widely appreciated that the future direction of markets cannot be predicted. What is known however is how markets are capable of behaving. This can be assessed simply by observing historical movements. Judging current patterns of price movement within the context of past market behaviour provides for greater confidence when market conditions become adverse. Hopefully acceptance will replace emotions of alarm and helplessness at times when markets turn south.

Let's explore the concept of risk further. There are several different types. The first to discuss is investment risk. This is the risk of receiving a poor return on invested funds. There are several ways that this can occur. At a company level a common cause is poor capital allocation by the company's management, resulting in either substandard returns or in the worst case scenario failure of the company and total loss of investor capital. Hopefully a skilled analyst would not have invested in this stock. However if you lack the skill, confidence or inclination to undertake individual company research you can significantly reduce your exposure to this risk by diversifying your portfolio. This would involve holding stock in several different companies which cover a range of business sectors. If you only have a small amount of money to invest then diversification can be achieved by investing in a managed or index fund.

The following discussion however is more about market risk. That is the risk associated with price change resulting from general market movements. Market risk has more to do with how investors behave when faced with market movement than it has to do with the movement itself. In this sense it could be termed a behavioural risk. Movement in "the market" is usually described by expressing the movement in the appropriate index. Whilst indices can be calculated for specific sectors of the market, in the absence of any qualification it is the general indices which are used to measure market movement. Examples of general indices are the Dow Jones or the S&P 500 in the United States, the Nikkei in Japan, the Financial Times Stock Exchange (FTSE) Index in the UK and the All Ordinaries Index or ASX 200 Index in Australia. So closely linked are the indices to each of their respective markets that the words are commonly used interchangeably. For example, when someone in the United States says "How was the market today?" they effectively mean "What was the points or percentage change in the Dow?" In Australia the same question would substitute for "What was the change in the All Ordinaries?"

As stated earlier there is an inordinate and at times unhealthy preoccupation with the reported market level. When financial reporters comment on the day's market movements they refer to upward movement in the indices as good news and downward movement as bad. But this seems rather strange. A downward movement of the market is not always a bad thing. If you have the intention to purchase a particular stock and its price has come down, not because of any specific company news but rather under the influence of general market movement, then this should be perceived as good news, not bad. Your entry price has just fallen. What is of significance is news specific to any of the companies which you currently hold or were intending to own. This is particularly so if the news indicates a material downturn in long term future profitability.

Yet the spirits of stockholders tend to be lifted by rising stock markets and lowered by falling markets. Financial wealth is measured by the ticker-tape rather than the real or the intrinsic.

You should always maintain discretion over when you buy or sell. You place yourself at significant risk when you surrender this control as is often the case when margin loan products are used to finance stock purchases. In using the stock portfolio as security for an investment loan you are exposing yourself to the risk of having to sell stock in the event of a material decline in general market prices. If the market value of the stock portfolio which you have put up as security for the loan declines below a predetermined percentage of the value of the loan itself then a margin call will be triggered. You will then need to either come up with more cash or sell stock. A failure to put up the cash will mean you will be forced to sell stock.

Liquidation of stock to meet margin calls is what exacerbated the rout of 1929 and is a common feature of bear markets including the crisis of 2008-09. In Fred Schwed's classic book, *Where are the Customers' Yachts?*, he summed up the predicament of the person who borrows on margin to invest in stock as:

"… the underlying principle may be loosely stated thus: buy them when they are up, and sell them when the margin clerk insists on it."

You must be free to choose when you buy or sell. Empowered by this discretion, market fluctuations should be of a lesser concern to you. If the market is low then you can choose to maintain your existing holding and look for buying opportunities. If the market is high then you may choose to maintain your existing holding or alternatively take the opportunity to sell part or all of your holding. You might take this latter action if a certain stock or stocks are overpriced by the market. A market at extremes provides opportunities.

By how much then do stock markets fluctuate? Is there a pattern or trend to their movement? Do good years follow bad or bad years follow good?

The fact is that no-one has ever demonstrated a capacity to predict future movements. If you accept this totally then you will not be alarmed when the market swings occur. Notable studies relating to past market movements have been undertaken by financial academics and market professionals such as Ben Graham, Jeremy Siegel, John Bogle, William Bernstein and Charles Ellis. Perhaps one of the most telling demonstrations of how stock markets fluctuate is the graphical representations of stock returns based on information provided by Jeremy Siegel and shown in Charles Ellis's book, *Winning the Loser's Game*.[44] Reproduced opposite, the first shows annual returns for US stocks between 1926 and 2000. It is representative of holding a diverse portfolio of stocks of similar construction to the index itself.

Fig. 1: S&P 500 annual returns from 1926 to 2000

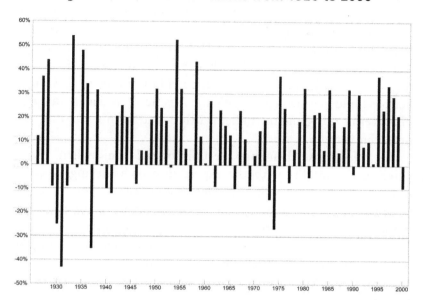

So significant is the potential of the above graph and the one following to the education of the reader that it is strongly recommended that time is taken to study them. A lot of information can be gleaned from the first graph. Striking is the extreme variability in annual returns. In any one year returns have varied from a gain in excess of 50 per cent to a loss of over 40 per cent. The staggering capital losses after the crash of 1929 can be seen clearly. Note however, that these years of loss were followed by some significantly positive years, one of which represents the highest one year advance on record. Note also that over the 75 year period one in four years is represented by negative returns and that there is no pattern to their occurrence. If you accept these facts and tailor your investment style to accommodate them then there should be no need for alarm when down years occur.

Let's return now to our discussion on risk and volatility. There is no doubt that the market is volatile. Annual variations in both market prices and stock returns are both wide and indiscriminate. If you hold a general portfolio of stocks for a period of only one year then you are exposing yourself to a wide range of possible returns. Since we can't predict stock market movements and there has historically been a one in four chance of the market delivering a negative return in any one year, then holding stocks for this short period could be likened to playing a game of Russian roulette. However in this game the bullet is being fired from a gun that has only four barrels!

It's no surprise then that the uninformed panic when, upon entering the market with the expectation of achieving positive returns, they actually experience negative returns. Unfortunately a common reaction is liquidation of their position at or near market lows. Yet in converting back to cash not only are they likely to be giving up good assets at depressed prices but they are failing to recognise that the chance of obtaining a positive return always was and would have continued to have been linked to the long term maintenance of their position.

In this circumstance it is not the market which is risky rather the investor's behaviour.

A very interesting thing happens when the period of holding stock is extended beyond one year. By way of illustration let's look at what the variability in returns would have been if a diversified portfolio of stocks had been held for various ten rather than one year periods over the same study period.

Fig. 2: Variability of returns on 10 year periods

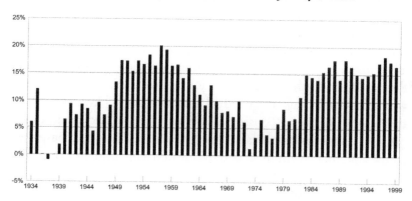

Over a 10 year time frame the chance of a negative return was dramatically reduced. And as the holding period decreased, there was an increasing tendency for returns to approach those represented by the one year graph. Consequently as the investment time frame decreased the chance of achieving a return either above or below the long term average increased. Accordingly the term "speculator" became increasingly appropriate to describe the behaviour of the stock owner as the holding period fell.

In terms of market downturns and their impact on investors let's look at an extreme event. And they don't come much more extreme than the stock market crash of 1929. The three years following this crash were devastating to stock portfolio values. From September 1929 to July 1932 the Dow Jones Industrial Average collapsed by 89 per cent. Anyone who came into October 1929 holding a portfolio financed by margin loans was wiped out — and many were. Following 1929 the public became so disenchanted with stocks that they were largely shunned as an investment vehicle. This, coupled with the fact that the market was overvalued in 1929, meant that it was a long slow climb for the market to regain the levels seen prior to the crash. American economist Richard Salsman summed it up when he said:

> "Anyone who bought stocks in mid-1929 saw most of his adult life pass by before getting back to even."

In fact the US market didn't return to nominal 1929 pre-crash levels as measured by the Dow Jones Index until late 1954. There are some very important points to make here. Firstly, and very importantly, Salsman's statement supposes that the person invested all of his money in a one-off investment decision in mid-1929 and then made no further investments for the rest of his life. This person would have to be one of the unluckiest investors to have ever walked the face of the earth. Consider if the same person had made a one-off investment three years after the 1929 crash. He would have seen a nine-fold increase in the market value of his investment from 1932 up until the same time target of 1954. But both examples are unrepresentative of typical investor behaviour. Investors are more likely to invest over time, effectively drip feeding money into the market.

Secondly, and again very importantly, investment returns should include reinvestment of dividends. It is from this activity that the real power in long term investment returns emanates. Reinvestment of dividends can also go a long way towards correcting capital losses and therefore shortening the period by which it takes for the investment to return into positive territory. On this basis it wouldn't have taken until 1954 for a one-off 1929 investment to return to its initial purchase price, rather it would have occurred in just over 15 years.

Since the typical investor invests in increments and because of the benefit to returns from reinvestment of dividends, let's reconsider how the investor would have performed if he had commenced the investment process at the market peak in September 1929. This time he places equal amounts of capital into stocks every month over a 30 year period and reinvests all dividends. Undertaking this activity for the period extending from 1929 to 1959 would have achieved an annual rate of return of 13 per cent. This far exceeds the 30 year returns achieved by those who believed they were clever by switching out of stocks and into cash or bonds at the time of the 1929 market peak.[45]

Consider now the situation of an investor who in 1929 had been reliant on the dividend flow from his stockholding to supply his income needs. He had no intentions of selling rather he looked upon his stock investments purely as a source of income. Would not he be concerned by the decimating impact on stock prices of the 1929 crash? Not necessarily, since if the companies of which he was a stockholder kept paying a consistent dividend, he should be indifferent as to the market's valuation of his stock.

Let's look then at what happened to dividends after the 1929 crash. It has already been stated that between September 1929 and July 1932 the Dow Jones Industrial Average fell by 89 per cent in nominal terms. Bob Shiller tells us that if the market fall was adjusted for changes in the cost of living over this period then it would be seen that the real (i.e. inflation adjusted) S&P Index fell 81 per cent between September 1929 and June 1932.[46] However, real dividends fell by only 11 per cent! This is not an isolated example. Shiller reminds us of another significant US stock market fall between January 1973 and December 1974. The real S&P Index fell by 54 per cent yet real dividends fell only by 6 per cent.

The reality is that markets tend to overshoot in both directions. A market typically crashes when stocks are overpriced but the fall stops when stocks are in oversold territory. Yet behind all this noise are the same companies plugging away daily doing what they have always done — whether it be mining or the production of goods and services. Sure, interest rates might be higher or demand for goods might be lower but the market usually overreacts to the impact that these factors have on long term corporate profitability.

The sentiments discussed in this chapter were succinctly articulated by Benjamin Graham in his classic book *The Intelligent Investor.*

> "... the bona fide investor does not lose money merely because the market price of his holdings declines; ... confusion may be avoided if we apply the concept of risk solely to a loss of value which is realised through actual sale, or is caused by a significant deterioration in the company's position..."

CHAPTER 18

A lesson forgotten

"The greatest mathematical discovery of all time."

ALBERT EINSTEIN

I was at primary school when first introduced to the concept of compound interest. Our teacher, by setting numerous mathematical examples, allowed us to compare the numerical outcome of the application of compound interest versus simple interest. No doubt examples demonstrating the benefits of compounding returns are commonly provided to tender aged school children throughout the world. But nearly as commonly the lessons, for most, have been forgotten.

Previous chapters might have left the initially enthusiastic investor dispirited with discussion of the prospect of achieving no better than average market returns. The novice investor commonly expects to achieve superior returns within short periods of time; anything less is considered pedestrian. It is time then to revisit primary school because the compounding of returns is the salvation of the average investor. It provides the turbo boost that converts the average into the exceptional. But the power it provides only works in the hands of the patient and the disciplined.

Let's first revisit what compounding of returns means. Consider an investor who deposits $10,000 into a bank account at 10 per cent interest. Every year he receives $1,000 in interest which is available for him to either spend or reinvest. If he spends the money his base capital will never grow beyond $10,000. Every year he receives and spends $1,000 until he eventually withdraws the initial principal. After 20 years he will still have $10,000 and he has received a total of $20,000 in interest payments. This non-reinvestment of returns is termed simple interest.

Consider now that he reinvests the interest each year rather than spending it. The reinvested interest now earns interest. The interest on the interest bears interest and so on. At the end of 20 years he will have a total of $67,250. The superior return is the result of compounding or reinvestment of returns. The power of compounding becomes magnified as the rate of return increases and period of time is extended.

As a practical example of the impact of rates of return on investment outcomes consider two separate one-off investments of $10,000 which are made for a 30 year period. One compounds at an annual rate of 7 per cent whilst the other compounds at the lesser rate of 5 per cent. In both examples all dividends are reinvested rather than spent so both are in keeping with the principle of compounding. The investment compounding at 7 per cent will grow to $76,122 after 30 years whilst the investment compounding at 5 per cent will only grow to $43,219 over the same time frame. Without the benefit of this calculation the uninitiated investor might have argued that a 2 per cent difference in annual return is minimal. The seasoned investor however would have calculated that this results in a 43 per cent reduction in the final payout figure.

Time is the friend of compounding and there are numerous stories and examples which demonstrate this fact. One classic demonstration is the story of how New York's famous Manhattan Island was acquired from the local Lenape Indians. In 1626 Peter Minuit, the then colonial governor of New Amsterdam (as today's New York was then referred to by the Dutch colonists) "bought" the entire island of Manhattan from the Lenape for 60 Dutch guilders worth of trinkets. Now, 1626 was long before US dollars were issued, but in 1846 historian John Romeyn Brodhead equated 60 Dutch guilders to about $24.

It is reported that the Indians had no concept of land ownership and consequently no understanding of what they were agreeing to. Nevertheless they accepted the beads and ribbons from the Dutch. The concept of purchasing 23 square miles of what was to become one of the world's most significant real estate holdings for a mere $24 might seem ridiculous until you calculate what $24 would be worth today, had it been invested and the returns allowed to compound. Had the Indians not accepted the trinkets but rather had placed the $24 in a Dutch bank at a modest 6.5 per cent rate of interest then the $24, with no addition to the initial principal amount, would have compounded to $763 billion by 2010. By 2010 the capital would have been growing by $127 million per day and by 2015 its total value would have surpassed $1 trillion.

Another favourite example of compounding is the answer to the question "Would you prefer to receive $1 million today or 1¢ today which will then be doubled every day for 30 days. The counter-intuitive but correct answer is the latter since 1¢ doubled every day compounds to over $10 million by the thirtieth day. Even starting with 1¢ and doubling it at the end of each month yields $687 million after three years. The amount is sizeable even though the 1¢ was doubled only 36 times.

The amounts achieved in the two examples presented above are both staggering. In the example of the Manhattan Indians the result is so large because of the significant time period over which the compounding is allowed to occur. In the second example it is the high rate of return that is being applied. They demonstrate that the investment returns achieved from compounding are impacted by both time and rate of return and therefore in order to maximise your investment returns you should apply both to your advantage.

Let's now turn to a more practical example. It uses a person who has a long term buy and hold philosophy. The trader or speculator is not considered in this example since their investment returns are less predictable.

The following example uses Jeremy Siegel's figures for real (i.e. inflation adjusted) returns for the US stock market. For the period 1802-1997 he calculated the real return on US stocks to be 7 per cent. For the post-war period from 1946-1997 he calculated the real return to be 7.5 per cent. Let's use the smaller return for reasons of conservatism. His figures assume reinvestment of all dividends. If you start with a seed amount of $10,000 and add an inflation adjusted $10,000 per year to the investment pool then in excess of $1 million (in today's money) will accumulate by the 30 year mark.

This level of saving can be achieved by a wage and salary earner but discipline is required. Whilst 30 years might initially sound a long time, a 50 year old will tell you that age 20 doesn't seem that long ago. Compounding a real rate of return of 7 per cent will result in a doubling of purchasing power every ten years. Hence even without the addition of any further money beyond the age of 50 this amount will grow to $4 million (inflation adjusted) over the following 20 years.

The above example uses quite conservative rates of saving. For the high income earner who starts with nothing but is capable of saving $50,000 per year, the inflation adjusted million dollar mark will arrive after 13 years and at 20 years the $2 million mark will be passed. If the same person had been investing for over 50 years, as has Warren Buffett, then applying only market average rates of return he would be worth $25 million at the 53 year mark. Remember that this represents today's spending power. Assuming a 3 per cent inflation rate, the actual non-inflation adjusted figure is $77.6 million not $25 million.

So for middle and higher income earners who have the potential to save these amounts of investment capital, financial independence is achievable within a relatively short professional career. Compounding, once understood, is the tool of the wealthy.

The use of these principles has enabled investor Warren Buffett to accrue a fortune. He has been investing for in excess of 50 years at rates of return far in excess of average market returns. Satisfied with a modest lifestyle, he has reinvested returns rather than consumed them. It is reported that Buffett's first wife Suzie spent $15,000 on house improvements at a time relatively early in his investment career. His comment to a pal was "Do you know how much that is if you compound it over 20 years?" At a rate of return of 24 per cent (which Buffett quite comfortably achieved), it would have amounted to $1.1 million. Expensive improvements indeed!

Considering the financial outcome of money invested versus the outcome of money consumed should not be a thought process unique to Warren Buffett. Any person who considers himself an investor should think this way. An investor assesses the future financial consequences of current decisions. Consider the following. In 1980 a new 280E Mercedes cost $30,000 if purchased in Australia. In 2007 it would have been worth approximately $3,000 if it was still on the road. Over a 27 year period it had fallen in market value by $27,000. The non-investor would tell you that the Mercedes cost the owner $1,000 per year and is likely to consider that to be cheap motoring. The investor, however, would tell you that if the $30,000 had been invested in the Australian stock market in 1980 and all dividends had been reinvested then the resultant stock portfolio would have been valued at $1 million in 2007. The investor sees the opportunity cost as the real cost — that is $1 million. But I hear you say that a car was needed and that even an investor needs to own one. Ask yourself then why it needs to be a Mercedes Benz. In 1980 a new Ford Falcon cost $6,000. The $24,000 price difference, if invested, would have meant that in 2007 the investor driving the Ford would also have owned a 27 year old car but in addition a stock portfolio worth in the order of $800,000. Apply similar thinking to multiple purchasing decisions and you can see why the accumulation of a significant body of capital is within reach of many individuals who otherwise would not have realised it.

CHAPTER 19

So, you need a recipe?

*"It usually takes a long time for investors
to become sophisticated enough to realise how
simple investing can be."*

PETER DI TERESA

Most novice investors expect to profit from their stock market activity by superior abilities in one or both of market timing or stock picking. In relation to the first, that is in terms of predicting the future movement of the general market, even great investors such as John Maynard Keynes, Warren Buffett and Peter Lynch deny that it is possible. The sooner would-be investors accept this, the sooner they can get on with the real investment process.

What then of gaining superior returns based on stock picking skills? The first misperception that should be knocked on the head is that superior returns can be achieved by selecting stocks based on "hot tips". This belief is particularly prevalent during bull markets when it appears that money is being made easily. In reality the only people who can guarantee a profit from acting on a hot tip are inside traders. They are typically company employees or members of the finance industry who are close to corporate deals such as takeovers, mergers and acquisitions. They profit from price sensitive information, acting on it before it becomes public and so before the market price of the stock has adjusted to the new information. They are not investors. Rather they are undertaking illegal behaviour and, if caught, face criminal charges. To consider this activity as synonymous with investing is like including a discussion on bank robbery in a book on how to boost your income. However, not all hot tips constitute inside information and the great majority are in fact best described as "hot air". The successful investor should follow a considered and disciplined plan of investment uninfluenced by rumour and hearsay.

What then the outcome of selecting stocks by a process of considered analysis? Does a comparison of earnings and dividend yields, relative management skills, social and economic factors and debt and financial structures provide an insight in picking superior stocks for investment? It would appear that the answer is yes and no. Let's explore this further.

Those investors who subscribe to the value school of investing put forward a strong case for the success of their stock picking skills. Ben Graham, Warren Buffett and Christopher Browne are but a few who have successfully built stock portfolios over time by purchasing undervalued stocks and holding them. Ultimately the general market recognises the true worth of the previously undervalued stock and bids the price up. But few people are able to emulate the success of the value investors. There are numerous reasons for this but the principal ones are that most people lack four fundamental characteristics that value investors possess. These four characteristics are patience, skill, discipline and faith. Let's explore each a bit further.

PATIENCE

A value investor is constantly looking for value that has yet to be recognised by the general market and therefore yet to be reflected in the stock market price. Or put another way, he purchases stocks that he believes, contrary to general belief, are underpriced. The return that he makes on his investment comes then from two sources. Firstly from future dividends and secondly from an upward movement in the stock price as its value becomes generally recognised. Returns from both these sources are usually not realised in the short term hence the value investor takes a long term view on his investments. Patience is a necessary characteristic.

SKILL

In any endeavour, excellence is required in order to achieve superior results. Mediocre input leads to mediocre results whether applied to sport, academia, business or personal relationships. Investment success is no exception. Superior investment success is the outcome of a mix of innate ability and a lot of hard work. Hard work cannot be ignored by anyone who wishes to achieve success. As brilliant as Michelangelo was, he is reported to have said "If people only knew how hard I worked to gain mastery it wouldn't seem wonderful at all." Donald Kendall, former CEO of PepsiCo, whilst less famous than Michelangelo, made an equally profound statement when he said "The only place that success comes before work is in the dictionary."

Great investors both past and present have demonstrated a mix of intelligence, passion and persistent application. The "average investor" is average due to a lack of one or more of these three qualities. It is obvious that not everyone can be above average and if you expect to be then be prepared to put in a lot of time and effort to achieve it. If you enter the market with the expectation that you are going to achieve superior returns, but with no substance behind your expectation, then be prepared for a very rude awakening.

By way of demonstration, let's look at how the market professionals perform. The term "market professional" is used to refer to the large number of people employed within the finance industry who aim to achieve above market returns with their capital allocation decisions. Part of this industry is associated with the accumulation and dissemination of investment advice. Represented by teams of economists, financial analysts, advisers and salespeople worldwide, you would expect these market professionals, who devote their working careers to the development of market related skills, to deliver superior investment returns to those who employ their services. Individually some might excel, but when considered as a group, they don't.

Let's consider firstly the source of the money which pays them. The simple answer is company profits. The money which pays them ultimately flows from the activities of the companies listed on the relevant exchanges. All the financial engineering, deal making and seemingly endless complexities associated with the peripheral activities of the stock market often don't actually generate any added value. On the contrary they represent a cost that is ultimately borne by the stockholders. Not only do stockholders have the last claim to any money flowing from company profits but they are usually standing at the end of a very long queue.

Here's where it gets interesting because it is possible to avoid some of these fees. The difference lies in whether you want to have your stock portfolio managed for you or whether you choose to manage it yourself. To have your stocks managed professionally can be undertaken several ways. A common way is to purchase units in managed funds. These funds invest money on behalf of investors and charge a fee for the service. The fee is taken from the dividend stream before the financial distribution is passed on to the unit holders. Typically the fee is in the order of one to two per cent of funds under management. Whilst on face value this doesn't sound much, when you consider that pre-tax dividend yields are commonly in the order of five to six per cent it can represent up to 30 per cent of the potential income stream. Of course this fee can be justified if the chosen fund manager delivers after-fee returns that are in excess of the market average.

Many investors aim to select a fund manager that will outperform either the market average and/or its industry peers. But there is no reliable technique for such a selection. Assessed within any given year the investment performance achieved by individual fund managers varies significantly. Yet when the group is considered as a whole, returns, after fees, approximate those of the relevant indices for the market in which they are operating. More significantly it is not uncommon for a fund which has recently provided below average returns to subsequently provide above average returns. For this reason it is best not to switch from one fund to another using recent performance as the principal criterion for selection.

Why fund managers as a group fail to outperform the market is distilled in the following quote from Charles D. Ellis:

"How can institutional investors hope to outperform the market ... when, in effect they are the market?"[47]

Investment returns aside there are several benefits to be obtained from placing your money into the hands of a fund manager. Four of the principal benefits are as follows. Firstly it does away with the need to make investment decisions for yourself other than, of course, selecting the fund manager in the first place. Secondly it reduces the administration and paperwork associated with managing your own investment portfolio. Thirdly it allows the small investor to achieve a level of diversification of his stockholdings that would not otherwise be possible. And fourthly fund managers are less likely to behave irrationally when financial markets start gyrating during times of excessive exuberance or pessimism. In this sense they act as a buffer between the emotional investor and the financial markets.

This latter point is particularly important when market sentiment is at extremes. Fund managers usually take the safe middle ground with investors' money. Consequently it is unlikely that they will achieve "Buffett-like" returns. But nor is it likely that they will take excessive risks with the money entrusted to them. They prefer to avoid an unconventional investment style, to not deviate too far from what their peers might be doing. Why they take this stance was expressed eloquently by John Maynard Keynes:

"If he is successful, that will only confirm the general belief in his rashness; and if in the short run he is unsuccessful, which is very likely, he will not receive much mercy. Worldly wisdom teaches that it is better for reputation to fail conventionally than to succeed unconventionally."[48]

Investors can also turn to boutique investment managers who charge a fee for making specific investment recommendations on their behalf. Rather than the purchase of units in a fund the personal manager will build a portfolio of stocks which are held directly by the investor. However, these services are usually offered to higher net worth individuals and fees tend to be quite expensive. Again, as a group, superior performance is not guaranteed. The use of boutique managers is best suited to high net worth individuals who are accepting of the high fees and who don't have the time or inclination to make investment decisions for themselves.

Management fees can be avoided if you are prepared to make your own investment decisions. For an investor with significant capital, a broad based portfolio of blue chip stocks can be acquired as a proxy to the general index. By spreading your investment dollars over a number of good quality companies which cover several sectors, a degree of diversification can be achieved. This will reduce the risk of substandard returns associated with holding an excessive weighting of stock in any particular sector or company. The use of this strategy should not assume that returns will be better than the market average.

DISCIPLINE AND FAITH

The two areas of investment which require discipline are the savings process and the investment process. The discipline associated with saving has already been discussed. With regard to the investment process there will be times when you question whether your investment plan will achieve the desired objective. These doubts are likely to be particularly strong at times when the prevailing market sentiment is one of pessimism. A significant market reversal will see your portfolio value eroded and under these circumstances you might be tempted to liquidate your stockholdings. This is most likely to be at the very time when it would be best to be buying. The most empowering emotion underpinning discipline is faith. Faith without education is best described as blind hope; true faith is derived from education and the establishment of a set of sound investment principles.

An investor's financial education can be taken to two levels. As a minimum, every investor must understand how financial markets can move. This knowledge must be developed to the level where market volatility is accepted as the normal course of events and where extreme market volatility, rather than arousing a sense of alarm, arouses a sense of opportunism. The investor who purchases units in a managed or index fund or establishes a broad based portfolio of blue chip stocks should, as a minimum, gain a financial education to this level.

The second tier of financial education is appropriate for the stock picker. The extent of this education is virtually limitless. The effort required to achieve an empowering level of faith within this investment arena makes it an exclusive club indeed.

THE RECIPE

Where then does this leave the average investor? Managed funds vary in their performance from year to year, but held over an extended period, they will most likely provide market returns. Investing in a few stocks can expose the small investor, who has limited capital, to higher than acceptable levels of risk. Diversification of direct stockholdings necessitates a larger pool of capital. Where do you start the investment journey with only limited capital and only a basic understanding of financial markets? Before this question is answered a further option needs to be discussed.

In 1949 John Bogle, a student at Princeton University, decided to look at the investment returns achieved by professional fund managers compared to the returns that could be expected from a portfolio based on the general market index. The former was represented by portfolios managed by market professionals, the latter by a passive investment approach requiring no research-based decisions but merely the construction of a portfolio that held the same stocks in the same proportion as those that made up the general market index. Bogle found that the fund managers, when considered as a group, failed after fees, to outperform the index. He concluded that if it is so difficult to outperform the market then why not be content to match it. Based on this finding Bogle formed the

Vanguard Group in 1974, and started the first of what are now many index funds. An investment in an index fund allows an investor to achieve a return that closely matches the associated index but doesn't outperform it. Using this approach allows diversification to be achieved even by the small investor. Fees are generally lower than those associated with managed funds as independent research isn't undertaken and stock switching is less prevalent. The portfolio mix is adjusted only in keeping with changes in the make-up of the index. This reduction in portfolio churning provides the added benefit of reduced transaction fees and capital gains taxes.

Ben Graham supported the use of an index approach:

"I have little confidence even in the ability of analysts, let alone untrained investors, to select common stocks that will give better than average results. Consequently, I feel that the standard portfolio should be to duplicate, more or less, the DJIA [Dow Jones Industrial Average]".

And this from Nobel Prize winner Paul Samuelson:

"The most efficient way to diversify a stock portfolio is with a low fee index fund. Statistically a broad based stock index fund will outperform most actively managed equity portfolios."

And if you need any more proof, this from Warren Buffett:

"Most investors, both institutional and individual, will find that the best way to own common stocks is through an index fund that charges minimal fees. Those following this path are sure to beat the net results after fees and expenses delivered by the great majority of investment professionals."

Index funds and also managed funds provide a simplicity that can be very attractive to the time poor investor. An additional benefit is that these funds accept investment capital in small increments, thereby allowing them to be linked to a regular savings plan. A commonly used savings and investment technique is "dollar cost averaging". Dollar cost averaging describes the investment of a fixed dollar amount made at regular intervals. In today's world of internet banking a regular automatic drawing can be made from a savings or cheque account directly into an index fund investment. This activity provides two significant advantages. Firstly it fulfils the need for discipline. If the drawing is automatic it requires no action by the investor. Excuses, temptation or absent mindedness are less likely to stand in the way of the savings and investment process. It fulfils the saving principle of "pay yourself first". If the money is not seen then it won't be spent. And secondly it overcomes the dilemma of market timing. Since the investment is regular and automatic there is no attempt to time the market.

Dollar cost averaging into an index fund or a managed fund is therefore a "recipe" which, if followed, should bring long term investment success. It brings together the principles of saving, discipline and diversification.

Part IV:
Enjoying Money

CHAPTER 20

In the minds of the wealthy

"Before we set our hearts too much upon anything, let us examine how happy those are who already possess it."

FRANÇOIS DE LA ROCHEFOUCAULD

French author and moralist François de La Rochefoucauld once reminded us that it is important to check how desirable a goal is before putting in too much effort to its pursuit. Considering the near universal desire for high levels of monetary wealth, it is worth looking at how those who have obtained it have found the experience. Indeed, to take the process one step further, if we find that they haven't benefited from it then it would seem foolish to pursue it, particularly if it undermines the enjoyment of life itself.

Identifying those who have amassed large fortunes is easy. *Forbes* magazine produces a list of the most "Wealthy Historical Figures". The list comprises 200 people placed in order from the wealthiest to the 200th wealthiest. Interestingly, entry to the list is not dependent upon being alive today. Meaningful comparisons between individuals are made by calculating the net worth of each as a percentage of the total gross domestic product of the nation they lived in at that time. The net worth of each can then be expressed in an amount that is a proxy for current day dollars.

Topping the 2008 list is J.D. Rockefeller with an adjusted current net worth of $318.3 billion. Not too far behind is Andrew Carnegie with $298.3 billion. Bill Gates is quoted as the wealthiest living person with $101 billion. Of course the list is not static, particularly amongst the living, but it is not the purpose of the present discussion to focus overly on the order but rather to provide a source of suitable people for consideration.

The first thing we notice is that wealth definitely doesn't provide an antidote to tragedy, illness or personal suffering. By way of example is oil billionaire Jean Paul Getty, who is number 46 on the *Forbes* list and was named in 1957 as the richest living American. He built this wealth in defiance of his father's predictions. His father, George Franklin Getty had little respect for his son. Just before his death in 1930, he predicted that his son would destroy the family company. A poor relationship with his father was not Jean Paul's only concern. During his life he was married and divorced five times. But perhaps the most tragic of life events for Getty was when on July 10, 1973 his grandson, John Paul Getty III, was kidnapped whilst living in Rome. The kidnappers demanded a ransom of $17 million be paid by Getty senior for his grandson's release. Getty refused to pay the money. The severity of the situation was then clearly spelt out when his grandson's ear was sent to a daily newspaper along with the threat of further mutilation if $3.2 million wasn't paid immediately. Getty ultimately obtained his grandson's release for approximately $2 million but lived with the stigma that the mutilation and associated emotional trauma could have been avoided if he had acted more promptly. The victim of the crime, John Paul III, developed a severe drug addiction following the event and in 1981 suffered a stroke which rendered him paralysed, speechless and blind for the rest of his life.

Getty's son Eugene Paul Getty (Paul Getty), father to John Paul III, was himself a drug addict who also suffered from chronic depression. Married three times, his second wife died of a heroin overdose in 1971.

Whilst Getty's life was one of personal turmoil, the life of Howard Hughes, listed as 52nd of *Forbes'* Wealthy Historical Figures, saw his life implode as the result of inner personal problems. Hughes is remembered not only as a wealthy American aviator, industrialist and film producer but also as an eccentric and a recluse. As a younger man he was a risk taker. It was perhaps this behaviour which led to a car, driven by Hughes, striking and killing a pedestrian named Gabriel Meyer in 1936. Hughes also suffered a long term addiction to opiates apparently used to control chronic pain resulting from flying-associated injuries. But Hughes' greatest problems came later in life. Suffering from a worsening obsessive-compulsive disorder, he was perpetually worried by potential cross-infection from other people. He withdrew from society, living his final years alone in a succession of hotel suites. He spent much of this time in bed watching movies. He cut his hair and nails only once a year. When he died in April 1976 at the age of 70, his 193 cm, 41 kg body was described as unrecognisable. Hypodermic needles were found to be embedded in the flesh of his arms and he was suffering from severe malnutrition.

Coming in at number 62 on the *Forbes* list of Wealthy Historical Figures is John Jacob Astor IV. He had inherited his $37 billion (value adjusted in 2008 dollars) as a legacy of his great grandfather, John Jacob Astor I, who had built a fortune based on fur trading and real estate. The family land holdings covered significant tracts of Manhattan Island. Despite his substantial wealth John Jacob IV's life was a tragic one. His first marriage, to Ava Lowle Willing, was an unhappy 18 years ending in divorce in 1909. They had shared little by way of common interest and Ava made it quite clear that she had little respect for her husband. In 1911 and despite his 47 years, Astor sought renewed happiness by way of marriage to 18 year old Madeleine Talmadge Force. Following an extended honeymoon in Europe and Egypt, the newlyweds boarded a ship in France for their passage back to New York. The ship was the Titanic. Whilst Astor's new (and pregnant) bride found refuge in a lifeboat, his lifeless body was retrieved from the Atlantic seven days after the Titanic sank.

Whilst not included in *Forbes'* list of Wealthy Historical Figures, the name Aristotle Onassis was one that was synonymous with wealth during the course of the twentieth century. Having made a fortune in shipping, he mixed with movie stars and presidents. But behind the glitz was a man who suffered significant personal tragedy. As a boy his life was at first privileged due to the benefit derived from his father's success as a businessman. But in the aftermath of World War I the substantial Onassis family holdings were lost. As a penniless refugee Onassis fled from Turkey to Greece. At about this time he lost three uncles and an aunt who were burned to death when the Turks set fire to a church in Thatira. In 1973, only two years before his death, the most tragic event in Onassis' life occurred. For a Greek, particularly a wealthy and powerful one such as Onassis, a son was perceived as part of one's self. Onassis looked upon his own son as a link to perpetuity; his beloved heir. However, on January 23, 1973 his only son Alexander Onassis died in a plane accident. Emotionally Aristotle never recovered.

It could be said that the tragedies born by Getty, Hughes, Astor and Onassis were personal and that they couldn't be linked to wealth. Certainly tragedy isn't dictated by the size of anyone's bank balance. It can equally affect poor or rich. But what the preceding does highlight is that wealth doesn't provide immunity to personal suffering.

An interesting study is the consideration of how wealthy individuals have perceived their fortunes. Has it changed their lives? Has it made them happy, content and fulfilled? Has it offered them something worthwhile, something that they otherwise might not have had? Or was it all a waste of time? Let's look at how two of the "king hitters" on the list felt about their wealth.

Fortunately we can gain an insight into how Rockefeller and Carnegie (number one and two on the *Forbes* list) felt about their fortunes because they expressed their feelings regarding this issue many times during the course of their lives. Let's then look at their perceptions and also at the behaviour of three other individuals who have qualified for *Forbes'* Top 200.

It would be timely to introduce Hetty Howland Robinson Green, better known as Hetty Green or "The Witch of Wall Street". Hetty, born November 21, 1834, was, at the time of her death in 1916, the wealthiest woman in the world. She comes in at number 41 on *Forbes'* list of Wealthy Historical Figures with an adjusted net worth of $58.8 billion. Despite her great wealth Hetty was despised by many and loved by few. She is remembered as much by her meanness as by her significant bank balance. Indeed the *Guinness Book of World Records* long had her listed as the "World's Greatest Miser". Of course it could be argued that how she spent her money was her own business but unfortunately there were times when her actions caused others to suffer.

Hetty received a significant inheritance from her wealthy father. The sum of $6 million in liquid assets derived from a lucrative family whaling business was left to her at age 30. Sixteen days following her father's death, Hetty's wealthy aunt died. Hetty was expecting to benefit from this event as well. However, much to Hetty's dismay her Aunt Sylvia had left over half her $2 million fortune to other relatives, friends, servants and charities. The remaining $1 million was to be invested so that Hetty could receive a lifetime annuity. The principal amount was deemed to ultimately pass onto other cousins both alive and as yet unborn when Hetty herself died. Hetty, however, wanted the lot and entered into a long legal battle to obtain it. She presented a document to the court which allegedly had been signed by her aunt and was aimed to renounce any will which benefited anyone other than herself. Three handwriting experts testified that the document presented by Hetty was a forgery. She lost the case but went on to multiply the $6 million that she had received upon her father's death into a fortune worth many times more.

Hetty's lack of willingness to spend money was legendary. Reported events include spending half the night looking for a mislaid two cent postage stamp and never turning on the heat in the depths of winter or using hot water to wash. Her wardrobe was sparse. It was reported that she would wear the same black dress until it wore out. Despite having a massive portfolio of assets, Hetty resented the thought of paying for an office. She worked rent-free from a corner of the Seaboard National Bank in New York.

Perhaps the most tragic outcome of Hetty's meanness was what befell her son Ned. Ned had, for a number of years, suffered a bad leg for which medical attention had been denied. However, the problem came to a head when 18 year old Ned sustained further injury to his compromised leg whilst returning home from an errand. A small boy riding in a wagon being towed by a St Bernard dog bowled him over, so further injuring the same leg. A few days later Hetty took Ned on the rounds of the free medical clinics around Brooklyn and Manhattan. These clinics were set up to serve the poor but Hetty, despite being the richest woman in the world, was hoping that her trademark old and worn black dress and Ned's second-hand under-sized suit would allow them to pass as paupers. Unfortunately for Hetty she was recognised at each of the clinics and after several days of failed attempts and with Ned's condition worsening, she was forced to pay for a consultation with a local physician. He recommended amputation above the knee. Hetty ignored the advice and attempted to treat the leg with home remedies. Despite significant periods of pain, Ned retained his leg for another two years until gangrene threatened his life. Ned's father intervened and ordered the leg amputated. The attending doctor declared that Hetty's tardiness had resulted in the need to amputate and that if the leg had been attended to in the first instance it most likely could have been saved. We don't know how Hetty felt about her lack of preparedness to spend the money necessary to save her son's leg but to any observer her actions speak louder than words.

And what became of Hetty's fortune? It was left to her two children Ned and Sylvia. Ned spent the greater part of his inheritance on extravagant living. Sylvia ultimately donated the bulk of her inheritance to charity. Had Hetty known how her fortune was to ultimately be distributed you can be sure that she would have been outraged.

The time frame of Hetty Green's life almost paralleled that of steel tycoon, Andrew Carnegie. Carnegie was born four days after Hetty's first birthday and died three years after she did. Carnegie was born in Dunfermline, Scotland and immigrated to the United States with his family when he was 12 years old. Since he spent the majority of his later life in New York, he no doubt crossed paths with Hetty Green.

Whilst Carnegie is now placed number two by *Forbes* magazine on the list of the world's most Wealthy Historical Figures he would have, had the list existed in 1901, been number one. The recognition of Carnegie as the world's wealthiest man occurred after Wall Street financier J.P. Morgan brokered what was at the time the world's largest ever corporate deal. The resultant company, US Steel, was formed from the amalgamation of several US steel companies with Carnegie Steel being the jewel in the crown.

Carnegie was a far more balanced person than Hetty Green. Sure he was a shrewd businessman but he was nothing like the miserly figure as represented by his fellow New Yorker. Carnegie fancied himself as a writer and left accounts of how he felt about his wealth. These writings provide a valuable insight into how someone in possession of such an immense fortune might perceive the benefits of having it.

Despite Carnegie amassing great wealth, he possessed a social conscience. In December 1868 at the age of 33 he penned a letter to himself. It was early in his career but he had already amassed assets totalling $400,000 which provided him with an annual income of over $56,000, a small fortune in 1868. The following words of introspection paint a man questioning his very own actions:

Dec. '68
St. Nicholas Hotel
N. York

Thirty three and an income of 50,000 per annum.

By this two years I can so arrange all my business as to secure at least 50,000 per annum. Beyond this never earn — make no effort to increase fortune, but to spend the surplus each year for benevolent purposes. Cast aside business forever except for others.

Settle in Oxford & get a thorough education making the acquaintance of literary men — this will take three years active work — pay especial attention to speaking in public.

Settle then in London & purchase a controlling interest in some newspaper or live review & give the general management of it attention, taking a part in public matters especially those connected with education & improvement of the poorer classes.

Man must have an ideal — the amassing of wealth is one of the worst species of idolatry. No idol more debasing than the worship of money. Whatever I engage in I must push inordinately therefore should I be careful to choose that life which will be the most elevating in its character. To continue much longer overwhelmed by business cares and with most of my thoughts wholly upon the way to make more money in the shortest time, must degrade me beyond hope of permanent recovery.

I will resign business at thirty five, but during the ensuing two years, I wish to spend the afternoons in securing instruction, and in reading systematically.[49]

Carnegie was the author of several social essays. In 1889 he wrote "The Gospel of Wealth", which outlined his belief that wealth was a public trust, that the money didn't belong to any one person.

He believed that his role was to allocate his wealth for the wellbeing of his fellow man and others who possessed wealth should do the same. The following words are quoted directly from his essay:

This, then, is held to be the duty of the man of wealth:

To set an example of modest, unostentatious living, shunning display or extravagance; to provide moderately for the legitimate wants of those dependent upon him; and, after doing so, to consider all surplus revenues which come to him simply as trust funds, which he is called upon to administer, and strictly bound as a matter of duty to administer in the manner which, in his judgement, is best calculated to produce the most beneficial results for the community.[50]

These were not hollow words. Carnegie lived his life in the manner he described. He donated his money to causes which he felt would provide lasting benefit to the community. The bulk of his fortune was used to build libraries and install church organs. He even believed that he could use his money to initiate world peace as futile as his efforts ultimately proved to be.

What then drove him to work and to build a steel empire if it wasn't for personal financial gain? It would seem that herein is the fundamental flaw — the assumption that he was doing it for the money. Carnegie's own words provide the answer. This is the entry into his diary made after the sale of his company in 1901:

"Trial bitter — father bereft of his sons — abandoned and alone — no more whirl of affairs, the new developments in — occupation gone. Advise no man quit business — plenty retire upon nothing to return to — misery."[51]

Therefore it was the process that provided enrichment in Carnegie's life — not the goal. And if it is the process which enriches a life then it is a profound mistake to endure an unsatisfactory process (read "unpleasant job") since the pot of gold at the end is simply no compensation.

Carnegie's mantle as the wealthiest man in the world started eroding after 1901. As he was rapidly donating his millions away, fellow American John Davison Rockefeller was continuing to build his fortune. Roughly the same age as Carnegie, Rockefeller was born when the Scot was a three year old boy.

Rockefeller's wealth was staggering. The 2008 inflation adjusted total of $318.3 billion has set a record yet to be eclipsed. The vehicle by which this was amassed was the company of which he was founder and chairman, Standard Oil. Standard Oil initially derived its profits from the production of kerosene used for lighting. However, it was the discovery and ultimately the widespread use of the internal combustion engine that projected his wealth into the stratosphere. As the electric light displaced the need for Standard Oil's kerosene, the internal combustion engine demanded its petroleum. Standard Oil, being the largest oil refiner in the world, was well placed to supply it. Rockefeller's surname became synonymous with the word wealth itself. How then did Rockefeller perceive his fortune?

As was the case with Carnegie, Rockefeller felt that it was a public trust. A religious man, Rockefeller believed that his role was to allocate the money temporarily provided to him by God for the benefit of others. In his late seventies he was quoted as having said:

"It has seemed as if I was favoured and got increase because the Lord knew that I was going to turn around and give it back."[52]

Rockefeller and Carnegie, whilst not personal friends, acknowledged each other's actions. Rockefeller sent Carnegie a note prompted when Carnegie funds allowed the establishment of a library in Pittsburgh.

"I would that more men of wealth were doing as you are doing with your money; but, be assured, your example will bear fruits, and the time will come when men of wealth will more generally be willing to use it for the good of others."[53]

It was clear that Rockefeller's motivation was not the pursuit of high levels of consumption. As was the case with Carnegie, the money came as a by-product of his activity rather than as a motivation in itself. This quote again from Rockefeller:

"I am convinced that we want to study more and more not to enslave ourselves to things and get down more nearly to the Benjamin Franklin idea of living, and take our bowl of porridge on a table without any tablecloth."[54]

Despite his bank balance, Rockefeller felt that a sense of personal wealth was determined by a set of inputs broader than money itself. He was quoted as saying:

"a man's wealth must be determined by the relation of his desires and expenditures to his income. If he feels rich on ten dollars, and has everything else he desires, he really is rich."[55]

So what did Rockefeller ultimately do with his money? Did he live up to his dissertations on stewardship and the need to pass it onto those less fortunate? Before his death he oversaw massive contributions to education, medical research and public health. By the time Rockefeller was in his eighties the Rockefeller Foundation was the largest grant-making foundation in the world. He gave away $530 million during his lifetime of which $450 million was directed towards medicine. The money continued to flow after his death in 1937.

So were the words in Rockefeller's note to Carnegie fulfilled? Has the time come "when men of wealth will generally be willing to use it for the good of others"? The examples set by Carnegie and Rockefeller have been emulated by some. Two present day proponents of the same philosophy are Warren Buffett and Bill Gates.

Buffett, as a successful investor, and Gates, as the founder of Microsoft, have traded places as the world's wealthiest living man. In June 2006 Gates announced that he would be stepping down from full time involvement with Microsoft so as to dedicate his efforts to the Bill and Melinda Gates Foundation, a charitable foundation aimed at improving standards in US education and reducing the prevalence of AIDS, tuberculosis and malaria in underprivileged countries. June 2006 also saw Buffett announce that he would contribute 85 per cent of his personal fortune to the Bill and Melinda Gates Foundation.

Buffett had long indicated that he would not leave a large inheritance to his children. The following quote appeared in *Fortune* magazine (September 29, 1986) where he stated that he would leave his children:

> "enough so that they would feel they could do anything but not so much they could do nothing".

Indeed Buffett himself could never be described as a member of the idle rich. At the time of writing he still works full time in his role managing Berkshire Hathaway. This is despite being 79 years old. Why is he still working?

The answer is simple. In his own words he "tap dances to work". As further evidence of his modest material requirements, Buffett still resides in the first house he purchased back in 1958. For Buffett, as has been the case of many billionaires before him, it is enjoyment of the process of life itself that is the principal driver of his actions not a pursuit of what the money can buy. He gains the respect of those around him not by a display of materialism but from a display of his acumen as an investor. The sum total of his assets simply serves as the score on the board, the score required to demonstrate his skill.

These examples deny the assumption that the super-rich are invariably driven by the pursuit of ever increasing levels of materialism. In fact, this type of behaviour is probably more typical of the middle classes. Maybe this is because the very wealthy have the opportunity to achieve a level of consumption which they feel comfortable with. Or maybe it's because they don't feel the need to display their wealth since it has already been widely acknowledged. They don't need to keep advertising the fact. Or perhaps the reason that they possess substantial monetary wealth is because they have always possessed the ability to live well within their means. These arguments do not deny that the level of consumption undertaken by some wealthy individuals can be by most standards extreme. But this behaviour appears to be more typical of those who have obtained the money either through inheritance or windfall.

Remember that there is no evidence to suggest that the lives of those who undertake high levels of consumption are better than those who have enough but have less. The message that must be remembered is that it is the process of doing and not the destination itself which is the source of personal satisfaction. The examples of Carnegie, Rockefeller, Buffett and Gates all lay testament to this. Consequently, in developed countries at least, you can gain as much fulfilment in life whilst scaling the bottom rung of the financial ladder as can be achieved whilst scaling the top rung. The important thing is simply to make sure that you are on the right ladder.

CHAPTER 21

What is wealth?

"Wealth is not about having lots of money. It's about having what we want. When we seek something we can't afford we are poor. Every time we are satisfied with what we have we may be counted as rich."

JEAN JACQUES ROUSSEAU

There are many objects that hold a similar meaning for all people. A coin is a coin is a coin. Equally the concept of a car a bicycle or a tree conjures up pretty much the same image in most people's minds independent of their race or social environment. Not so the word "wealth". Wealth is a perception not an object. This is what complicates its definition. The interpretation of the perception of wealth is as varied as the number of minds that attempt to perceive it. It is a concept sculpted principally by the social environment within which that mind operates. It is therefore not surprising that definitions of wealth vary. The *Webster's Dictionary* defines it as:

"The value of one's total possessions and property rights."

The *Oxford English Dictionary* defines wealth as:

- "An abundance of valuable possessions or money."
- "The state of being rich."
- "An abundance of something desirable."

The last definition is the one that is open to the broadest interpretation since it doesn't necessarily imply material possessions or money as the measure of wealth. It allows you to define what the object of desire is. There is no point in a definition that quantifies wealth. There is no point in saying that someone is wealthy when they have one million dollars or ten million dollars. It is all relative. Who is the person perceiving this wealth? For a person in a subsistence economy, wealth is likely to mean sufficient food and shelter. For a person in Bel Air, Los Angeles, wealth may mean a 200 square mansion and an eight-figure bank balance. A broader definition may have nothing to do with material possessions at all. Wealth can be described in terms of health, wellbeing and quality of life. This concept of wealth was put forward by the English critic and writer John Ruskin. Ruskin believed a country is wealthiest that nourishes the greatest number of happy and noble human beings — "There is no wealth", said Ruskin, "but life including all its powers of love, joy and of admiration." This definition, unlike a materialistic one, is applicable within any social context.

In further exploring the concept of wealth consider the following. There are approximately six and a half billion people presently living on planet Earth. Of these, one and a half billion (approximately one-quarter) exist on less than a dollar a day. In terms of its position on the economic ladder, 94 per cent of the world's population live in countries economically poorer than Australia (as measured by GDP per capita). This means that six per cent of the world's population live in an environment that provides them with a higher GDP per capita than Australia. The bulk live in the United States, home to five per cent of the world's population. But anyone who has spent time in both Australia and the United States could quite easily argue that there is little difference between these two countries in terms of economic wealth. Therefore it could be stated that Australians, as a group, live in a country that is amongst the most economically prosperous in the world.

Yet many residents of Australia would not appreciate this fact. It is common to hear people complaining of their unsatisfied needs. We describe "the Aussie battler" who is struggling in his day-to-day existence, often in debt and never seeming to be able to rise beyond anything except a state of financial desperation. He might be "doing it hard" when compared to some other Australians but what if he was transported to a shanty town in Manila or to a starvation-ridden community in Rwanda or Tanzania? The Aussie battler would be wealthy beyond the Tanzanian's wildest dreams.

Very few look to cross border comparisons. Most fall victim to petty comparisons between themselves and those around them. The friend's new car, the neighbour's new kitchen, the brother-in-law's superior salary all become a source of comparison with little regard to the fact that their own circumstances are good as well.

At the commencement of chapter 4 it was stated that economist John Stuart Mill recognised this in his comment that:

"Men do not desire to be rich but richer than other men."

Mill's observation strikes at the heart of the problem. As long as an individual seeks financial wealth using a definition that relies on comparison with other men then he will forever be dissatisfied. Only the world's wealthiest man could say that he has achieved the goal under the terms of such a definition. Yet so many people travel through life using this as their governing goal.

It is worth restating the quotation from the start of this chapter. Eighteenth century French philosopher Jean Jacques Rousseau acknowledged the futility of this behaviour when he said:

"Wealth is not about having lots of money. It's about having what we want. When we seek something we can't afford we are poor. Every time we are satisfied with what we have we may be counted as rich."

You would therefore be better placed to use the *Oxford English Dictionary* definition of wealth as "an abundance of something desirable" and to self-articulate an achievable definition for "something desirable". It would be non-comparative. The definition would stand alone and be independent of what others thought, what they have and what they think they need.

Jean Jacques Rousseau described in his book *Discourse on the Origin of Inequality* the phenomenon that primitive people were content because they were unaware of what they didn't have. Or put into a modern Western context, how could you covet your neighbour's BMW if BMWs didn't even exist?

In your attempts to achieve investment success these social tendencies should be recognised. Rule number one should be that you are not undertaking the process of investment in order to compete against the world. Don't enter into a game that has no goals, no parameters, where enough is never enough. In a journey that has no destination each step is closer to nowhere. Where consciousness is directed towards those with more yet is blind to those who have less. This contest will never be won. A definition of wealth must be established that works for you. Goals can be monetary but not open-ended. The underlying motive is not driven by materialistic indulgence rather the pursuit of being able to spend time as you wish. American author Christopher Morley defined what he believed to be success when he stated:

"There is only one success: to be able to spend your life in your own way."

Yet most people don't do this. They spend their lives conforming to an economically defined norm as they emulate those around them.

How then should the definition of wealth be set? Morley's definition of success is a good starting point. For certainly as mortal beings our life is limited by time and we should be endeavouring to make every part of it count. It is useful to combine Morley's definition of success with the *Oxford English Dictionary's* definition of wealth to establish a personalised definition of wealth such as:

"Sufficient passive income so that the need for money doesn't define how I spend my day."

An investor with this definition would, rather than pursuing an indefinable amount of money, actually have something to work with.

What is the size of the pool of capital required to deliver an income stream that negates the need to work? The size of that income stream and therefore the pool of capital required to deliver it is defined by the recipient and his family. The cost of that lifestyle is quantified at the outset and is best assessed in light of current financial needs. The investor then sets in place a programme to accumulate that amount of capital which will provide the predetermined level of passive income. Whilst adjustments to this figure are able to be made during the course of the capital accumulation process, excessive upward adjustments risk the target ever being met.

Under this definition of wealth a person having established a level of passive income that fulfils their economic needs will not have a working life dictated by an endless stream of external controls. This is a person who could cease work tomorrow with no alteration to his economic wellbeing. Work then becomes a choice. It is maintained only if it is enjoyed.

Herein lies the key to investment success. Before the journey commences the successful investor knows what is to be achieved and why.

CHAPTER 22

The Greeks tried to tell us

"People are about as happy as they make up their minds to be."
ABRAHAM LINCOLN

The journey is by no means complete. Let's assume that you have been able to earn, save and invest a sufficient body of capital to support yourself and your family. Now you have come to the most important part — enjoying it. Potentially this discussion could be kept short since it is appropriate to state that very little by way of income is required in order to live a fulfilling and enjoyable life. It could be stated that once basic levels of food, shelter, clothing and education are taken care of then whether you are happy or not is independent of financial factors. In reality material possessions beyond these basic needs have but a fleeting impact on our level of happiness. Indeed The New Testament made this point very clearly:

> "There is great gain in godliness with contentment; for we brought nothing into the world, and we cannot take anything out of the world, but if we have food and clothing, with these we shall be content."
>
> First letter of Paul to Timothy,
> Chapter 6, Verses 6, 7, 8. The New Testament

Once we are fed, clothed, warm and healthy the factors that impact on our degree of happiness and fulfilment have more to do with interpersonal relationships and levels of self-esteem and self-worth. We know that these factors don't require a large bank balance for their fulfilment. But comment won't be left here because if the obvious is merely stated rather than explained then it will be treated by the reader as a motherhood statement that is quickly forgotten. For despite people being reminded that high levels of materialism are not a prerequisite for a fulfilling life, high levels are still pursued with a widespread fervour that shows little sign of abating. Indeed this was recognised by John Stuart Mill 160 years ago when he observed that America (except in the South) had attained an advanced state of wealth and political freedoms but that:

"All that these advantages seem to have done for them is that the life of the whole of one sex is devoted to dollar-hunting and of the other to breeding dollar-hunters."[56]

The theme of this book has been about investment. For those with a dollar-hunting mentality the subject is of interest. But what to do with those dollars once obtained is the issue. This book is not about consumption or materialism. As the title states it is about *Creating Real Wealth*. The question needs to be posed. Is there another cause served by the capital accumulation and the investment process? Is there another reason why we might undertake the process of investment?

Many people would respond initially to this question with a sense of incredulous bemusement. So deeply instilled within our society's belief set is the notion that it is desirable to accumulate as much money as possible that few would question it. Most believe that more is better in the same way that they believe the world is round and that Sunday follows Saturday. Yet everyone, and the budding investor is not excluded here, should ask what is the aim of their activity.

For thousands of years, academics, thinkers and philosophers have put their minds to the question of what is the underlying motive of any of life's activity. Almost invariably consideration turns to the pursuit of happiness and personal fulfilment as the ultimate aim. In relating this to the subject of this book, most people would perceive this as the reason why they wish to accumulate capital. They believe that more money will automatically bring increased levels of happiness. They believe that money, through the purchase of material symbols of status, will attract attention and acceptance from others. In addition, by arousing the emotion of envy in those around them they so raise their own levels of self-esteem.

But these beliefs need to be challenged. For if it turns out that they aren't true then the investor who mindlessly spends his entire life chasing this goal will end up bitterly disappointed. So much of our lives are spent living the more-is-better philosophy that little time is left to question it. But the concept has been challenged for some time. The ancient Greeks are acknowledged as spawning some great philosophers who put their minds to this very question.

Socrates (470-399 BC) was an early advocate of independent thought. He didn't require confirmation in order to form an opinion. He challenged the concept that the majority was always correct and espoused the concept that the truth was more likely to come from critical and logical thought than blind acceptance of common opinion. Fifty-eight years following the death of Socrates another independent Greek thinker and philosopher, Epicurus was born. Epicurus put his mind to what factors brought happiness into your life. He felt that people were looking in the wrong place and interestingly his thoughts are as relevant to modern man as they were when he articulated them nearly 2,500 years ago.

Epicurus felt that what we needed in order to live a happy life could be distilled down to three fundamentals: friends, freedom and living a considered life.

FRIENDS

There is currently a popular author and financial commentator who has released a number of books proposing techniques that can be used for financial advancement. In an appearance on American cable channel CNBC he proposed that one technique for financial advancement is to only associate with people who are financially successful. He went on to say that if your friends are "losers" (in a financial sense) then it would be best to cease associating with them and to look for a new set of "friends". What this commentator fails to recognise is that this belief denies true friendship. Those who look upon people merely as vehicles to assist in the pursuit of personal financial gain should be pitied, for it is likely that any interpersonal relationships they have will be particularly shallow.

FREEDOM

Epicurus's second requirement for the establishment of a happy life was the need for personal freedom. He felt that life was more likely to be enjoyed if it was independent of outside controls. This concept is not a foreign one. Animals of the wild live in their natural habitat, owning nothing. And we often envy them their freedom.

It is the minority of humans who are independent of outside controls. Most either work for a boss or have self-imposed financial constraints that control how they spend their day. They load themselves up with debt and then spend the rest of their lives working in order to repay their financial commitments. Freedom has long since been relinquished.

A CONSIDERED LIFE

Analysis of your life involves time out from routine to reflect on worries and concerns. Removing yourself from them, even for a brief time, assists in putting them into perspective. Epicurus felt that anxieties diminish if you allot time to thinking things through. Few people provide themselves the opportunity for this to occur. They fill their lives with activity and give little consideration to whether their activity is fruitful or futile. They are just too busy being busy and don't ever lift their heads up to see where they are going.

Despite being provided with the capacity for independent thought, most people make no attempt at self-analysis, rather they voluntarily comply with mass belief. American social critic Lewis Mumford is credited with the following:

"With all our super-abundance of energy, food, materials, products there has been no commensurate improvement in the quality of our daily existence. The great mass of comfortable well fed people in our civilisation live lives of emotional apathy and mental torpor, of dull passivity and enfeebled desire, lives that belie the real potentialities of modern culture."

In deriving his determinants of a happy life, it should be remembered that Epicurus lived in a very different age. Whilst the concepts he espoused are still relevant and applicable to man's current social situation, it should be remembered that there was a different emphasis on how time was spent then compared with now. Today there is a greater emphasis on work. It has assumed a higher importance in most people's lives, and consumes a greater proportion of our waking hours. Commensurate with the increased preoccupation with work as an activity, perhaps we should add a fourth determinant of happiness and so extend Epicurus's list to that of spending your working time pursuing a worthwhile goal or ideal.

As already quoted, but I think it bears repeating, John Stuart Mill summed this up well when he said:

"Those only are happy who have their minds fixed on some object other than their own happiness — on the happiness of others, on the improvement of mankind, even on some act or pursuit followed not as a means but as itself an ideal end. Aiming thus at something else they find happiness by the way."

The achievement of the goal brings a short-lived satisfaction but it is the pursuit of a meaningful goal that helps achieve long-lived happiness. Put another way: it is not the pursuit of happiness rather the happiness of pursuit.

The example of Andrew Carnegie well illustrates this point. For Carnegie work was not purely a means of amassing money. He ultimately lived for the process of work itself. It is important to consider this point since worthwhile pursuit can be undertaken at all stages of life not just within your working career. Financial self-sufficiency provides choice and with choice greater flexibility is available to pursue a worthwhile goal. Some fortunate people are able to pursue such a goal within the context of paid work. These people see their work as having true meaning. The work is in alignment with their own goals. They are stimulated and satisfied by their work and are likely to undertake this activity independent of the salary. But for most people work merely provides a means of financial support for themselves and their family. It is often tolerated only through self-imposed necessity. For these people financial independence would open the door of choice. They could spend their time as they wished pursuing a goal of their choosing, independent of whether it was paid or not.

By intertwining concepts of investment with philosophical beliefs, it is possible to answer the question "Why invest at all?" Why accumulate capital? In answering this question let's refer back to Epicurus's tenets. Note the absence of materialism in Epicurus's list of what constitutes a happy life. The presence of friends is independent of money. An analysed life requires time and thought not money. Freedom in our society requires money but it doesn't require displays of materialism. That financial freedom is so elusive for many has more to do with high expectations than it has to do with economic reality. People's financial expectations often have no bounds hence financial independence, for these people, as defined by the absence of the need to work, is never going to be achieved. And even for those who might be able to place a cap on their material expectations, if the cap is too high then the amount of capital required to fulfil them might be too difficult to amass.

For those people who have boundless, unachievable financial expectations the answer to the question "Why invest at all?" is probably best answered, "Don't bother". No amount of money will ever satisfy them.

Why then invest? Invest with the aim of achieving financial independence. Financial independence will facilitate the achievement of Epicurus's concept of a fulfilled life. It will free up time to spend with family and friends. It will negate the need to submit to the will of others as is the case when a living needs to be "earned". It will allow time for self-analysis, balance and the pursuit of activities that are enjoyable and fulfilling.

Financial goals are best intertwined with the attainment of personal ideals not as a means of facilitating consumption. If your aim is purely to obtain as much money as you can so as to buy all which shines and glitters then you have lost the investment game before you even started.

CHAPTER 23

Forget the Joneses

"You wouldn't be as concerned about what other people think of you if you realised how seldom they do."

ANONYMOUS

The key to success in managing personal finances at every level is to forget the Joneses. Whether you are making, saving, investing or enjoying your money it is essential to have an independence of thought and mind that provides immunity to the thoughts and actions of those around you. In setting goals for income there is little to be gained from envying those who earn more since it is likely that they won't be putting their income to good use. What's more it is likely that you can achieve what you want with what you currently earn. To facilitate the process of saving don't fall prey to the corrosive activity of using your income to purchase the same items that those around you have in the endless game of "keep up". When investing have a Socratic mindset that guides decisions from the basis of considered and logical analysis rather than blindly and emotionally following the crowd. And when it comes to enjoying life pursue goals that you define yourself, not by basing them on prevailing social attitudes.

It is difficult for many to say goodbye to the Jones family, for they set the benchmark by which everyone wants to judge their achievements. The reason we look to any benchmark is to facilitate the emotions of self-esteem and peer group acceptance. But it is essential to realise that both of these emotions are best served through non-monetary avenues. So earn by way of a job you enjoy, save a proportion of what you earn, invest wisely and without emotion and enjoy life by pursuing self-determined dreams.

REFERENCES

1 Keynes, John Maynard, *The General Theory of Employment Interest and Money*, Macmillan Cambridge University Press, 1973 [1936].

2 Veblen, Thorstein, *The Theory of the Leisure Class*, Penguin Books, 1994 [1899].

3 Dominguez, Joe and Robin, Vicki, *Your Money or Your Life*, Penguin Books, 1992.

4 Hill, Napoleon, *Think and Grow Rich*, Frederick Fell Publishers, 2002 [1937].

5 Mill, John Stuart, *Autobiography*, Penguin Classics, 1989 [1873].

6 Posner, Michael, "Whatever Happened to Spare Time? The Protestant Ethos in Turmoil, or Why We Can't Stop Working", *World Press Review*, Vol. 38, September 1991.

7 Stanley, Thomas J. and Danko, William D., *The Millionaire Next Door*, Pocket Books, 1996.

8 Venti, Steven and Wise, David, "Choice, Chance, and Wealth Dispersion at Retirement", NBER Working Paper No.7521, February 2000.

9 de Tocqueville, Alexis, *Democracy in America*, Translated by Henry Reeve, Cambridge, Sever and Francis, 1863.

10 Veblen, Thorstein, *The Theory of the Leisure Class*, Penguin Books,1994 [1899].

11 Maslow, A. H., "A Theory of Human Motivation", *Psychological Review*, 50, 1943.

12 Klein, Naomi, *No Logo*, Flamingo, Harper Collins Publishers, 2001.

13 Schopenhauer, Arthur, *The Wisdom of Life and Counsels and Maxims*, Digireads.com, 2008.

14 Mill, John Stuart, *Principles of Political Economy with Some of Their Applications to Social Philosophy*, 7th Edition, Longmans, Green, Reader and Dyer, 1871.

15 Keynes, John Maynard, "Economic Possibilities for our Grandchildren" in *Essays in Persuasion*, W.W. Norton, New York, 1963.

16 Mill, John Stuart, *Principles of Political Economy with Some of Their Applications to Social Philosophy*, 7th Edition, Longmans, Green, Reader and Dyer, 1871,

17 Diogenes of Oinoanda, *The Epicurean Inscriptions of Oinoanda*, Translated by M. F. Smith, 1993.

18 Mill, John Stuart, *Principles of Political Economy with Some of Their Applications to Social Philosophy*, 7th Edition, Longmans, Green, Reader and Dyer, 1871.

19 Hamilton, Clive, *Growth Fetish*, Allen & Unwin, 2003.

20 Thoreau, Henry David, *Walden; or, Life in the Woods*, Forgotten Books.

21 Siegel, Jeremy, *Stocks for the Long Run*, 2nd Edition, McGraw-Hill, 1998.

22 Gibson, George, *The Stock Exchanges of London, Paris, and New York*, G.P. Putnams & Sons, New York, 1889.

23 Bachelier, Louis, *Theory of Speculation: The Origins of Modern Finance*, Princeton University Press, 2006, [1900].

24 Keynes, John Maynard, *The General Theory of Employment, Interest and Money*, Macmillan Cambridge University Press, 1973 [1936].

25 Graham, Benjamin, *The Intelligent Investor*, 4th Edition, Harper and Row Publishers, 1973.

26 Ibid.

27 Shiller, Robert, *Irrational Exuberance*, Scribe Publications, 2000.

28 Band, Richard, *Contrary Investing for the '90s*, The Investment Library, 1989.

29 Carswell, John, *The South Sea Bubble*, Sutton Pub Ltd, 1993, p.120.

30 Walsh, Justyn, *The Keynes Mutiny*, Random House Australia, 2007.

31 Morgan, John, *The Life and Adventures of William Buckley*, Archibald MacDougall, 1852.

32 Graham, Benjamin, *The Intelligent Investor*, 4th Edition, Harper and Row Publishers, 1973.

33 Kelly, Fred, *Why You Win or Lose — The Psychology of Speculation*, Dover Publications, 2003 [1930].

34 Buffett, Warren, Letter to Partners, January 18, 1963.

35 Buffett, Warren, Berkshire Hathaway Annual Meeting, 1987.

36 Kelly, Fred, *Why You Win or Lose — The Psychology of Speculation*, Dover Publications, 2003 [1930].

37 Odean, Terrance, "Are Investors Reluctant to Realise their Losses?" *Journal of Finance*, 1775-98, 1998.

38 Siegel, Jeremy, *Stocks for the Long Run*, 2nd Edition, McGraw-Hill, 1998.

39 Greenberger, Martin, *Computers, Communications and the Public Interest*, The John Hopkins Press, 1971.

40 Seldon, G. C., *The Psychology of the Stock Market*, BN Publishing [1912].

41 Ibid.

42 Dreman, David, *Contrarian Investment Strategies: The Next Generation*, Simon & Schuster, 1998.

43 O'Shaughnessy, James, *What Works on Wall Street*, 3rd Edition, McGraw-Hill, 2005.

44 Ellis, Charles D., *Winning the Loser's Game*, 4th Edition, McGraw-Hill, 2002.

45 Ibid.

46 Shiller, Robert, *Irrational Exuberance*, Scribe Publications, 2000.

47 Ellis, Charles D., *Winning the Loser's Game*, 4th Edition, McGraw-Hill, 2002.

48 Keynes, John Maynard, *The General Theory of Employment, Interest and Money*, Macmillan Cambridge University Press, 1973 [1936].

49 Krass, Peter, *Carnegie*, John Wiley & Sons, 2002.

50 Carnegie, Andrew, *The Gospel of Wealth*, Signet Classics, 2006, [1889].

51 Krass, Peter, *Carnegie*, John Wiley & Sons, 2002.

52 Chernow, Ron, *Titan*, 2nd Edition, Vintage Books, 2004.

53 Ibid.

54 Ibid.

55 Ibid.

56 Mill, John Stuart, *Principles of Political Economy with Some of Their Applications to Social Philosophy*, 7th Edition, Longmans, Green, Reader and Dyer, 1871.

FURTHER READING

Part I: Making Money

Hill, Napoleon, *Think and Grow Rich*, Frederick Fell Publishers, 2002 [1937].

Nightingale, Earl, *The Essence of Success: The Earl Nightingale Library*. Vols 1-10, CD Collection. Nightingale-Conant Corporation.

Stanley, T.J. and Danko, W.D., *The Millionaire Next Door*, Pocket Books, 1996.

Part II: Saving Money

De Botton, Alain, *Status Anxiety*, Penguin Books, 2004.

De Graaf, John, Wann, David and Naylor, Thomas, *Affluenza*, 2nd Edition, Berrett-Koehler Publishers, Inc., 2005.

Dominguez, Joe, Robin, Vicki, *Your Money or Your Life*, Penguin Books, 1992.

Hamilton, Clive, *Growth Fetish*, Allen & Unwin, 2003.

Hamilton, Clive and Dennis, Richard, *Affluenza*, Allen & Unwin, 2005.

Schor, Juliet, *The Overspent American*, Harper Perennial Publishers, 1999.

Part III: Investing Money

Investor Psychology

Barach, Roland, *Mind Traps — Mastering the Inner World of Investing*, Dow Jones-Irwin, 1988.

Dreman, David, *Psychology and the Stock Market*, Warner Books, 1979.

Kelly, Fred, *Why You Win or Lose*, Dover Publications, 2003, [1930].

Keynes, John Maynard, *The General Theory of Employment, Interest and Money*, Chapter 12, Long-Term Expectation, Macmillan Cambridge University Press, 1973, [1936].

Le Bon, Gustave, *The Crowd, A Study of the Popular Mind*. Cherokee Publishing Company, 1982, [1895].

Neill, Humphrey, *The Art of Contrary Thinking*, The Caxton Printers Ltd, 1976 [1954].

Nicholson, Colin, *The Psychology of Investing*, Wilkinson Publishing, 2006.

Nofsinger, John, *Investment Madness*, Prentice Hall, 2001.

Selden, G.C., *The Psychology of the Stock Market*, BN Publishing, [1912].

Zweig, Jason, *Your Money and Your Brain*, Souvenir Press, 2007.

Market Panics — Booms and Busts

Chancellor, Edward, *Devil Take the Hindmost*, Plume (Penguin Group), 2000.

Dale, Richard, *The First Crash — Lessons from The South Sea Bubble*, Princeton University Press, 2004.

Gleeson, Janet, *Millionaire*, Simon & Schuster, 1999.

Kindleberger, Charles, *Manias, Panics, and Crashes*, 4th Edition, John Wiley & Sons, 2000 [1978].

Lowenstein, Roger, *When Genius Failed — The Rise and Fall of Long Term Capital Management*, Random House, 2001.

Mackay, Charles, *Extraordinary Popular Delusions and the Madness of Crowds*, Crown Trade Paperbacks, 1980 [1841].

Menschel, Robert, *Markets, Mobs & Mayhem*, John Wiley & Sons, 2002.

Investing

Band, Richard, *Contrary Investing for the '90s*, The Investment Library, 1989.

Dreman, David, *Contrarian Investment Strategies: The Next Generation*, Simon & Schuster, 1998.

Ellis, Charles D., *Winning the Loser's Game*, 4th Edition, McGraw-Hill, 2002.

Graham, Benjamin, *The Intelligent Investor*, 4th Edition, Harper & Row, 1973 [1949].

Graham, Benjamin and Dodd, David, *Security Analysis*, 5th Edition, 1988 [1934].

Malkiel, Burton, *A Random Walk Down Wall Street*, W. W. Norton, 1996 [1973].

Nicholson, Colin, *Building Wealth in the Stock Market*, John Wiley & Sons Australia, Ltd, 2009.

O'Shaughnessy, James, *What Works on Wall Street*, 3rd Edition, McGraw-Hill, 2005.

Shiller, Robert, *Irrational Exuberance*, Scribe Publications, 2000.

Siegel, Jeremy, *Stocks for the Long Run*, 2nd Edition, McGraw-Hill, 1998.

Part IV: Enjoying Money

Tycoons and Business Mogels

Chernow, Ron, *Titan. The Life of John D. Rockefeller, Sr.*, 2nd Edition, Vintage Books, 2004.

Drosnin, Michael, *Citizen Hughes*, Broadway Books, 1985.

Fraser, N., Jacobson, P., Ottaway, M., Chester, L., *Aristotle Onassis*, Weidenfeld and Nicolson, 1977.

Krass, Peter, *Carnegie*, John Wiley & Sons, 2002.

Lenzner, Robert, *Getty — The Richest Man in the World*, Grafton Books, 1987.

Lewis, Arthur, *The Day They Shook the Plum Tree*, Buccaneer Books, 1963.

Schroeder, Alice, *The Snowball — Warren Buffett and the Business of Life*, Bloomsbury, 2008.

Slack, Charles, *Hetty — The Genius and Madness of America's First Female Tycoon*, Harper Perennial, 2005.

Philosophy

De Botton, Alain, *The Consolations of Philosophy*, Penguin Books, 2000.

INDEX

inside traders 153
intelligence 87, 88, 110
Intelligent Investor, The 79, 84, 94,
113, 147
interest rates 139
International Monetary Fund 25
internet bubble 102
internet companies 91
internet stocks 92, 98
intrinsic value 83
investing 35, 87
investment 94, 95, 158, 187
– advice 155
– loans 38
– returns 129
IQ 88, 95
irrational behaviour 80

Jackson, Michael 22-24
James, William 10, 47
John the Baptist 63
Joneses, the 42, 189
Joplin, Janis 15
Journal of Business 76

judgments 132
Kahneman, Daniel 132
Karl, Harry 20
Kelly, Fred 114, 125, 126
Kendall, Donald, 155
Keynes, John Maynard ix, 36,
52, 53, 56, 58 78, 79, 83, 121,
153, 157
Keynes Mutiny, The 110
King's College Chest Fund 79
Klein, Naomi 47
knowledge ix, xi, 138
Kuznets, Simon 56
La Psychologie des Foules 108
Lamborghini 22

Latin America 24
Law of Large Numbers 131
Law, John 99, 100
Le Boeuf, Michael 60
Le Bon, Gustave 108, 109, 110
Legrance, Joseph Louis 88
Lincoln, Abraham 182
listed property trusts 66
"Living with Michael Jackson" 23
Long Term Capital Management
(LTCM) 93, 94,133
Los Angeles 178
Louis XIV 99
Louisiana 100
Lownsberry, Thomas R. 96
luck 124
Lynch, Peter 118, 127, 153

Mackay, Charles 97, 101, 104
managed funds 139, 156, 157, 159,
160
management 154
management fees 158, 160
Manhattan Island 149-150, 170
Manila 24
margin calls 141
margin lending 106, 107, 145
margin of safety 86
market
– behaviour 134, 139
– cycles 117
– experts 117
– exuberance 91, 106, 107
– movement 141, 143
– pricing 77
– professionals 155
– timing 118
– value 80
Maslow, Abraham 46
Massachusetts 63

ACKNOWLEDGEMENTS

I would like to acknowledge those who assisted me during the pre-publishing phase of this book. Firstly those who read the manuscript and provided constructive comments regarding its structure and content. My friend, Grant Riddell, provided comments which led me to restructure some of the early chapters. Colin Nicholson and Harry Stanton also read the manuscript. Colin, who had been through the process of publishing several times before, provided me with some invaluable advice about the process itself. Thanks also to Harry Stanton whose comments provided me with further encouragement to proceed with the endeavour.

Thanks also to my son Andrew who used his skills in graphics to produce the charts seen on pages 143 and 145. And also to my wife Sandra and daughter Jessica whose interest in the project helped me during the process.